Lew Wallace

The Wooing of Malkatoon

Commodus

Lew Wallace

The Wooing of Malkatoon
Commodus

ISBN/EAN: 9783743441798

Manufactured in Europe, USA, Canada, Australia, Japa

Cover: Foto ©Lupo / pixelio.de

Manufactured and distributed by brebook publishing software (www.brebook.com)

Lew Wallace

The Wooing of Malkatoon

MALKATOON

The Wooing of Malkatoon

Commodus

By *Lew. Wallace*
ILLUSTRATIONS BY
Du Mond & Weguelin

LONDON AND NEW YORK
HARPER & BROTHERS PUBLISHERS
1898

CONTENTS

	PAGE
THE WOOING OF MALKATOON	3
COMMODUS	83

ILLUSTRATIONS

MALKATOON	*Frontispiece*	
"AND I WILL TELL HIM OF OUR OTHMAN BOLD" . . .	*Facing p.*	4
"I REMEMBER WELL THE DAY"	"	12
OTHMAN IN NO MAN'S LAND	"	20
"OTHMAN IN HIS STIRRUPS ROSE"	"	58
OTHMAN HAS A VISION	"	74
"THIS BAITING THOU SHALT RUE"	"	98
"WHAT, GOOD MY LORD, UPON MY KNEES?"	"	114
CLEANDER READS THE LETTER	"	120
THE SINGING BACCHANTES	"	132
"YES OR NO—SPEAK! IS THERE ANOTHER LIFE?" . . .	"	156
DEATH OF MATERNUS	"	166

THE WOOING OF MALKATOON

PROLOGUE

CHILD MÁHOMMED[1]

The dance and song, the tales and juggleries,
With which the wise Sultana-mother used
To speed the laggard hours of harem life,
Were good for folk with souls of every day;
But Máhommed would nothing have that did
Not stir his warrior sense. The cymbal's crash,
And trumpet's strident notes, unmixed of plaint
Or melody, could always bid him near
And hold him fast, a wild-eyed listener;
And with his urchin's fist he beat the drum,
And trembled with delight to hear its roll
Invade the silent places of the house,
And die in distant halls. And all day long,
With a heap of stippled ivory cubes,

---

[1] Máhommed, the son of Sultan Murad II., frequently called Amurath. Upon the death of his father, Máhommed succeeded to the Sultanate as Máhommed II., and after the fall of Constantinople surnominally he added *The Conqueror* to the title.

The gift antique of a forgotten prince
Who erstwhile ruled a land of elephants
Off in the sunrise somewhere, he would build
Tall castle piles, and wall and moat them round,
And when he thought them perfect for defence,
Retire a little space, and with his bow
And arrows shoot them into formless wrecks.
But best of all he loved of afternoons,
When, in the musky-shaded central court,
The ladies of the household met to feast
On spicèd meats, and nuts, and snow-cooled draughts,
And exchange trinketries and quips as rich,
And chorus loud the while the slaves before
Them spread what all the merchants from the gates
Without had dared to send them — such the time
The doughty child best loved to dight himself
As Eastern knights for battle bound were wont,
And on the Kislar-Aga's sword for steed,
And yelling shrill, with undissembled rage
And fury burst upon the startled groups,
And send them screaming thence, and, doing so,
Imagine that he did but re-enact
The rôle of black Antar, who used alone
To sheer ten thousand horsemen of their heads.
Nor were there any of the luresome wiles
With children potent since the world began
Enough to lay the martial jealousy
With which he held the court. Nor cared he more

"AND I WILL TELL HIM OF OUR OTHMAN BOLD"

PROLOGUE

For truce proposed in form by heralds trained,
And leading troops of buglers clad in gold,
And blowing flourishes until the sky
Were like to crack and fall. At length would come
The high Sultana. In her deep reserve
Of mother-love she held the only charm
To calm his mood and raise the well-kept siege.

"The battle's done. My lord must now dismount;
And I will tell him of our Othman bold,
And how he wooed and won his Malkatoon."

And with the saying she would gravely reach
Her hands to him, and he would run to her,
And at her feet throw down his lance and shield;
And haply seated then, his ruddy cheek
Soft pillowed on her twin-orbed, ample breast,
The tale she would unfold.

I

EDEBALI THE DERVISH

                        " My lord must know
That in the ancient time, near Eskischeer,
A many-gated town, there dwelt a Sheik,
Edebali by name. A chambered cave
He had for house, and wild vines made his door,
Which was a nesting-place for singing birds.
Two paths, divided by an olive-tree,
Led from the door: one to a spring of cool,
Sweet water bubbling out from moss-grown rocks,
And it was narrow; while the other, broad
And beaten, told of travel to and fro,
And of the world a suitor to the man,
For it is never proud when it has need.
He had been Sheik in fact, but now was more—
A Dervish old and saintly, and so close
To Allah that the Golden Gate of Gifts
Up Heaven's steep did open when he prayed.
Wherefore the sick were brought him for a touch;
And in their crowns his amulets were worn
By kings and queens, and scarce a morning came

THE WOOING OF MALKATOON

Without a message—' In my tent last night
A foal was born to me, and that in truth
It grace its blood, I pray thee send a name
To know it by.' Or, from a knight whose brand
Had failed him, ' Hearken, O Edebali!
Thou knowest by chosen texts to temper swords.
The craftsman hath a new one now in hand,
And in the rough it waits.' And men of high
Degree came often asking this and that
Of Heaven, and the Prophet, and the laws
Of holy life. Nor was there ever one
To go away unanswered, for he knew
The Kur-án, verse and chapter, and to speak
With finger on the line

II

OTHMAN AND MALKATOON

"And to the cave
Our Othman often went, because he knew
The good man loved him. Once he thither turned
While hawking and athirst, and at the door
Bethought him of the spring. So down the path,
The narrow path, he went, but sudden stopt—
Stopt with the babble of the brook in ear,
And straight forgot his thirst in what he saw.
Below the fountain's lip there was a pool
O'er which a mottled rock of gray and green
Rose high enough to cast the whole in shade;
And in the shade unconscious sate a fair
And slender girl. A yellow earthen jar,
Which she had come to fill for household use,
Stood upright by her, and he saw her face
Above a fallen veil, a gleam of white,
Made whiter by the blackness of the hair
Through which it shone. And she, all childlike, hummed
A wordless tune of sweet monotony,
As in the hushed dowar at dead of night

THE WOOING OF MALKATOON

The Arab women, low-voiced, sing to dull
The grinding of their mills. And to her knees
Her limbs were bare, and as the eddies brought
The bubbles round she beat them with her foot,
Which glistened mid the splashes like the pink
And snow enamel of a sea-washed shell;
And by the throbbing of his heart he knew
Her beautiful, and turned and walked away,
Himself unseen. And up the path he went,
A stately youth, and tall, and self-contained
As any proven man.

III

OTHMAN AND EDEBALI

                 "'A quest I bring,
O saintly Dervish!' Thus, when in the cave,
Our Othman spake.

                 " The elder to him turned
His face benignant.

                 "'Is there in the Book¹
A saying that would make it sin for me
To marry?'

                 "'Nay, son, speak thou whole of heart.'

"'Then be it whole of heart,' young Othman said,
'And to thy saintliness.' And stooping low,
He raised the other's hand, and kissed it once,
And then again, and humbly. 'At the brook
But now I saw thy daughter Malkatoon—
Nay, be thou restful!— Drink for soothe of thirst

        ¹ The Kur-án.

Was what I sought. Her presence made the place
In holiness a Mosque, and bade me off,
And I ran trembling here. And that which was
Not more than thirst is now a fever grown,
A fever of the soul. And if I may
Not wed her, then it were not well to let
My morning run to dismal noon of life;
Nor shall it. See, now, O Edebali!
Here at thy feet my soul. Save Malkatoon's.
Thou canst not find one whiter.'

"And he knelt,
And laid his forehead lowly in the dust;
And at the sight, Edebali made haste,
And both hands helpful raised the suppliant,
Saying, 'O gentle son of Ertoghrul!
What Allah of his love and bounty gives,
That we shall keep, and in the keeping make
Our care of it becoming thanks and praise.
Thou knowest I love thee'—

"His farther speech
Was tearful.

"'I remember well the day
A woman beautiful, and mine in love
And wifely bonds, and dying of the birth,
Gave me her baby, saying, I have named

It Malkatoon,' and as thou dost by it,
So Allah will by thee. Ah, verily!
The Prophet measureth the very show
Of evil 'gainst the good; and dost thou think
It full enough with Him that I have kept.
The child in bread and happy singing all
The morning through, if now, her noon at hand,
I give her up to certain misery?
A prince art thou, and she but dervish born;
And men will laugh, and with their laughter kill.'

"And to and fro he walked, and wrung his hands,
While all the lineless wrinkling on his face
From thought, and fast, and vigils long endured,
The deeper pursed itself; and when he stopt,
It was to say, 'To Allah let us leave
The judgment, prince. Who dares in Him to trust
May always hope. So canst thou hither bring
A pigeon from an eagle's nest escaped
Unruffled, or a lamb that overnight
Hath harmless lain with lions, it will be
As speech to me, and I will do His will.
Knowest thou the Legend on the seal of God?
Our lives are but the wax on which 'tis stamped.
They call it Kismet.'

"And with that he drew

¹ Treasure of a woman.

THE WOOING OF MALKATOON

His robe, long, loose, and trimmed with yellow fur,
About him close, and left the youth alone
And wonder-struck, but none the less in love.
Then down the broad and travel-beaten road
Our Othman, pensive, went to where his train
Of tribesmen waited.

IV

OTHMAN AND HIS TRIBESMEN

"' Ho, now! Hood the hawks,
And leash the whimpering hounds. The day is done.'
Thus he to them.

"They stared, and in his palm
One whispered, 'Oh! It is the evil eye.'

"A bolder spake, 'My lord, it is but noon.'

"And yet a third addressed his hunter's love
In strain more cunning, 'Has my lord forgot
The heron in the marsh?'

"But he, low-voiced
And patient, answered them, 'Nor hawk, nor hound,
Nor heron more for me, for I have seen
A lily with a star's light in its cup.
'Tis something by the breath of Allah blown

THE WOOING OF MALKATOON

This way from Paradise, I swiftly thought,
And all impulsive would have made it mine
But that a voice forbade; and now I go
To find what never mortal eyes have seen—
A pigeon from an eagle's nest escaped,
Or in a lion's den a lamb alive.
So on my breast the lily I may wear,
And in my heart the star's light.'

"Then their eyes
Were hot with dew of tears repressed by awe.
For strangers to the sweet delirium
Which only lovers know, and know to make
The gentle-hearted gentler, and the brave
More covetous as errants in the Land
Of the Impossible, they thought him mad;
And at his feet one wistful flung himself,
With outcry, 'I was born to serve my lord,
And go with him.'

"Whereat the others drowned
His voice with theirs united, 'And so were we.'

"But Othman waved them off: 'Bring me my horse.
But yesterday from noon to set of sun
He kept the shadow of the flying hawk
A plaything 'neath his music-making feet.
I will not comrade else.'

OTHMAN AND HIS TRIBESMEN

"Tent born and bred,
The steed was brought, its hoofs like agate bowls,
Its breast a vast and rounded hemisphere,
With lungs to gulf a north wind at a draught.
Under its forelock, copious and soft
As tresses of a woman loosely combed,
He set a kiss, and in its nostrils breathed
An exhalation, saying, to be heard
By all around, 'Antar, now art thou brute
No longer. I have given thee a soul,
Even my own.'

"And as he said, it was,
And not miraculously, as the fool
Declares; for midst the other harmonies
By Allah wrought, the hero and his horse
Have always been as one.

"And when they saw
Him in the saddle, face and eyes aglow
With the low-burning, splendor-chastened flame
That serves the Angel of the pallid wing
In lighting martyrs on their rueful way,
They closed around him, and of their charms
And priceless amulets despoiled themselves,
And tied them on Antar until his mane
And forelock jangled as with little bells,
And glistened merrily, though all the time

The true men moaned, 'Oh! Oh! What shall we tell
The good Sheik Ertoghrul?"

                    "And in reply,
He bade them, 'Say that I to-day have learned
The Legend graven on the seal of God,
And that it is a holy law in need
Of holy lives to prove it.'
        [1] Othman's father.

V

OTHMAN IN NO MAN'S LAND

                                        " Thereupon
He rode away, clad all in hunter's garb,
And all unarmed, save at his belt a sword,
And at his back a shield—into the East
He rode bareheaded, and under a sky
Thrice plated with molten brass of noon,
Nor once looked back. Into the Wilderness,
The far and purple-curtained distances,
Where Nature holds her everlasting courts,
With beasts of prey and hordes of savage men
To keep their portals, questionless he passed
In leading of his faith.

                                " And to a land
Of lions come at last, of all he met,
Even the women at the black-tent doors,
He asked if lately they had lost a lamb?
And where the tawny thunder-makers kept
Their dread abodes? Or if they knew the cliffs
Whence through the many-folded turbaning

THE WOOING OF MALKATOON

Of sun-touched clouds the nesting eagles launched
Themselves upon their prey? For he had heard
From Allah that 'twas beautiful to love
All helpless things, and shield them from their foes,
And therefore was he come.
                              "And all the men
Who heard him laughed; the women, pitying,
Were moved to tears, and gave him of their stores,
And at his going blessed him. And in time
He came to know the trails the manèd brutes
Affected most, and lay in wait to see
With what of trophies of their craft they took
Their homeward ways. Or on some barefaced rock,
The sky above him like a stainless blue
Pavilion, prone and patient he would watch
The winged Sultans of the aërial world
As forth they issued screaming to the sun,
Which at the call seemed, comrade-like, to stand
And wait for them. And well he came to know,
When from their forays provident they flew,
The victim in their talons. If a bird,
He whistled to his horse, and followed them
With loosened rein. And where they thought their nests
Securest in their envelopes of cloud
And dizzy height, he thither boldly climbed
And gave them battle.
                         "Thus into a year
The months slow-melting fell, and he became

OTHMAN IN NO MAN'S LAND

A hero; so that, went he here or there,
All living things remarked him. Did men see
A troop of eagles circling in the sky
They smiled, and said, 'Our Othman this way comes.'
And mothers, from their midnight slumbers roused
By lions, closer clasped their little ones,
And calmed them, whispering—'Hush! and sleep again!'
For gallop, gallop goes the gray-black steed,
While Allah swings the moon-lamp overhead.
And Othman, strong-armed, rides, and riding cries,
'Be still, O baby-hearts, be still, and sleep,
For I am here.'

           " And 'gainst the friendly folk
Who loved him so there one day chanced to come
A horde of camel-drivers, skurrying
From parched Oasian orchards in the South.
To them sweet water was of more account
Than blood of women. Then from far and wide
The harried residents to Othman drew
For guidance, and he led them never knight
More truly. And the battle done and won,
In league and gratefully, as warriors should,
They flung the clashing of their steel-bossed shields
Into the upper deeps, with rhythmic stops
For outcry. 'Hear, O Allah!'—thus they said—
'The Wilderness hath travailed, and to-day
A Tribe is born to Thee. Thy palm is large,

And hollowed roomfully, and lined with gifts
For all who couch their asking in the form
Of humble prayer.' Thus Kara[1] Othman saith;
And, as there is no fervid friend like him
Of helpless things, who—who shall better speak
To us of Thee, or better serve the Tribe,
So in its new birth blind? Then live the Sheik—
Sheik Othman! Live the Tribe!'

[1] *Kara* means Black. Othman was so called from his raven beard and hair.

VI

OTHMAN RENEWS HIS PRAYER FOR MALKATOON

"And when the spring,
The second of his love-lorn wandering,
Was pluming all the land, our Othman rose,
And with the chosen of his just-fledged Tribe,
A motley train of wild men, homeward rode,
And coming to the cave where yet the sage
And saintly Dervish dwelt, 'Is it not time,'
He said, full risen from his low salaam,
'That love like mine should have surcease of test?
Behold what it has done!'

"And from his breast
He drew a double string of eagle beaks,
Each amber-hued and set with polished gold,
And clear as honey from the comb thrice pressed
Into a crystal cup.

"'Thou didst require
Of me a bird—dost thou remember it,
Edebali? It was to be a sign

THE WOOING OF MALKATOON

From Allah, so thou saidst. Nor that alone—
Right well I knew thy purpose by the task
To try my faith, and find if well or ill
The Prophet held me. Wherefore be thou judge.
These were the blades with which the Kings of Air
Were wont to rend the hapless feathered tribes,
And keep their blue domain. Upon their thrones
I slew the monsters. Count them if thou wilt,
And take the trophies, trinkets now to please
A maiden fair. Perhaps young Malkatoon
Will wear them; only when thou comest to put
Them in her hand—which in my dreams I kiss,
The many thousand times I dare not say—
I pray thee tell her how the gift was won,
And fairly speak my name. Then if she smile,
And ask of me, and why I dared such deeds,
And what love is—ah, more than well enough!
As singing birds in hush of summer nights,
Calling their mates through green acacia groves,
Have answer in the self-same melody
Of speech, so she will love me for my love.'

The Dervish stayed his hand. 'It was a bird
I asked of thee, my son—a living bird—
A pigeon'—

    "'Nay,' said Othman, patiently,
'I have no bird.'

"'Oh, then thou hast the lamb?'

"'Nor lamb have I. Yet, saintly though thou art,
Be not in haste, as saying, "All the ways
Are Allah's, and I know them."'

"Answering
The sign he made, a servant brought a bale
Of lion skins, and cast it on the floor,
And spread the pelts to view; and they were soft
To eye and touch as rugs of Indian silk,
Yet terrible withal, for each retained
The head with all its armature of teeth,
And bulk of yellow mane, the jaws agape
And snarling.

"'These were royal draperies,
Good Dervish, yielded to me but with life.
And when I took them, it was with the thought
That thou, for whom all things, the quick and still
Alike, have tongues, wouldst kindly hear them tell
Of Allah's love for me, and ask not more
Of sign from Him. And scarce less sweet it was
To think that when their tale was haply told,
They might find favor with young Malkatoon;
And should she hear it said the hand that won
The necklace from the eagles was the hand
That spoiled the lions thus, and all for love,

THE WOOING OF MALKATOON

As carpets on her stony chamber floor,
Or dressing for her couch such days and nights
As chilly blow the mountain winds, they might
Well keep me in her mind, and even nurse
A wish to learn yet more of that which drove
Me to the errantry. And now thy hand?—
And graciously, I pray. A crown were reft
Of half its honor did the giver give
It grudgingly. No? Oh, I see! It is
Because these witnesses are in their speech
Uncertain. I have better. Wilt thou go
And hear them?—Only to the door; they wait
Us there.'

"And to the vine-clad door they went,
The old man in the leading of the young;
And looking out, lo! cumbering the road,
In the white noon, and plainly not yet used
To bonds of lawfulness, a medley blent
Of lowing cows, and camels malcontent
And overladen, hungry, wolf-like dogs,
And travel-stainéd sheep, else spotless black,
And horses beautiful enough for kings,
And by their owners far more loved than were
Their youthless wives, mere handmaids of the brutes—
In the noon, lo! the Tribe.

"'Came these with thee?'
The Dervish asked.

OTHMAN RENEWS HIS PRAYER FOR MALKATOON

"And Othman, pleased to mark
His wonder, smiled, and said, 'I am their Sheik.
The Wilderness hath rendered them to me,
And they are Prophets now.'

"Then, half in quest
And half in scorn, the elder's brow and hand
Impulsive rose. But Othman meekly bowed,
And answered, patient still, 'Ah me! They were
So true thy words the day I boldly asked
The hand of Malkatoon: "For men will laugh,
And with their laughter kill." In other phrase,
The jesting critics in my father's halls
Would make a plaything of her simple soul,
And drive it weeping back to Paradise,
With none to know how lavishly of charms
And all perfections it was clothed on,
Save thou, and I, and Allah. And the thought
Went with me down into the No Man's Land,
Whither I betook myself companionless,
A question ever present, How to keep
My love the child she is, and harmless save
Her from the courtly brood? At last I had
An answer. You must know the land was wild,
Uncastled, townless, and the people dwelt
Apart as enemies, and ruthless preyed
Upon each other, making mock of love
And Allah; and when I shewed them trust

THE WOOING OF MALKATOON

They laughed at me, and let me go in peace,
A dreaming madman. But in time there came
A hopeful change. By what 'twas wrought I leave
The necklace and yon bale of robes to tell.
Out of the farther South there one day rose
A cloud of war with grim necessities
They knew not of before; and it blew fire
Upon them, and calamities so fierce
They came to me, and in large charity
I yielded to their prayer, and ordered them,
And with them took the field. And as we charged
I shouted *Allah! Allah!* And they caught
The holy name, and with it swung their swords,
And aimed their lances, all so joyously,
It seemed the blood they shed had turned to wine,
And made them sudden drunk. We won the fight,
And they are Moslem now. Then as I sat
My horse the children and the women came
And kissed his bloody front, and caught my hand
And stirrups, painted with the same red drip,
Proclaiming, Live Sheik Othman! And the men
Made answer, Live Sheik Othman! Then a new,
Exquisite pleasure wrapt me in a glow
Of strange delight, and, looking up, I saw
The moon a crescent in the day-sky's depth,
And by it, lustrous clear, the star assigned
To wait on it, as page upon a queen.
Some childish thought—a wonder if the sun

OTHMAN RENEWS HIS PRAYER FOR MALKATOON

Were not enough to show the havoc strewn
Along the field — was passing through my mind,
When suddenly the face of Malkatoon
Appeared to me, a fleck of brighter light,
Resilvering the silver of the moon.
I raised my hands as worshippers are wont;
I could not speak, for all my senses swam
In dim confusion; and before I woke
The apparition drew the coarser rays
Of star and planet round it, and was veiled
From sight. And when 'twas gone, I knew myself,
By certain intuition of the soul,
In Allah's care. I knew that Malkatoon
Would be my wife. I knew the warrior-cries
For me as Sheik was Allah making known
What He would have. Wherefore, behold my Tribe—
The Tribe of Othman! Prophets of the State
Which I will build with them! And as thou lovest
His officers, the little and the great,
Look kindly on them, father, for they know
Right well to follow where I dare to lead.
And think'st thou they will laugh at Malkatoon?
Or wound her gentle soul with glance or speech
Unseemly? Nay, good Dervish, say the word,
And here before thy door the Tribe shall pitch
My great black tent and set the wedding-feast,
And hold it on with story, meat, and drink,
And merry joust, until the new year come,

THE WOOING OF MALKATOON

Unless thou sooner say that never bride
Had truer welcome to a truer home.
I ask it—I, Othman—who never prayed
To other man.'

"And then the Dervish said,
Slow speaking, ' To my cave there often come
Ambassadors of kings, and yesterday
The high Sultan of ancient Samarkand
Saluted me in person royally,
And in his shower of gifts my feet were hid,
Or had I stept, it would have been on pearls
And precious stones; and yet more welcome thou,
O son of Ertoghrul, than all of them—
A messenger from Allah with the key
He keeps upon the door above the vault
Where things to come lie hidden' gainst their day—
Take thou salute, and hear, then go thy way.
The wise man reads the name of Allah writ
On everything in Nature—on the stone,
The wasting leaf, the glittering water-drop—
And comes at last to look for prophecy
In all the unaccounted trifles strewn
By chance along the blind-worn paths of life.
These trophies are not voiceless as they seem.
I listen, and they tell me of the East
By thee again restored and masterful;
I listen, and they tell how turbaned hosts

OTHMAN RENEWS HIS PRAYER FOR MALKATOON

Devout shall come from every land to light
The ready torches of their faith at thine;
I listen, and from out the upper depths
I hear a voice declare thy name shall be
Forever on the lips of fighting men
A battle-cry, and that in times of peace
Even the winds, unsteady passengers
And lawless though they are, shall take and blow
It up and down the world a melody
Of bugles. Up—up to the storied plains
Of glory thine forewritten 'tis to climb;
And bending ear, and listening wistfully,
I hear the music thence of horns and drums,
And cymbals ringing, and the high acclaims
Of countless men in arms; and if I look,
It is at thee enthroned on battle-fields,
And conquered cities crowding with their keys
On golden plates, and clamorous to buy
Thy better will. And yet, alas! I dare
Not speak the word besought. In truth, it is
Thy destiny I fear. When greatness cloaks
Thee like a tabard more than courtly dight,
What then of Malkatoon? Mayhap, 'twill be
For me, O son of Ertoghrul, to seek
A lion's den or eagle's nest for lamb
Alive or dove unharmed, and fail as thou
Hast failed. A question—one; then peace to thee,
And all of thine. Where doth that holy thing,

A trusting woman's simple love, fare worst?
And I will tell: 'Tis in the heart by years
Of kingly usage into marble turned—
Thou hast my answer.'

                "And with that he took
The young man's hand in both of his, and held
It tenderly, as loath to let him go
So sadly burdened; then when he had back
His voice, he said, 'The Wilderness hath· kept
Itself unlocked, and rendered thee the Tribe
In sacred trust for Allah; whence 'tis thine
To wait on it, and bend its stubborn will
To honor Him. The truest blades are those
Most frequent in the fire, and thus may He
Be chastening thee. Thy faith to this hath been
In purity like pearls in Heaven's gate.
Forget not now that all the times are His,
The morrows and the years, in which to send
The sign I ask.'

             "He turned, but at the door,
The inner door of heavy camel's-hair,
He left the parting speech. 'A woman dead,
And in her grave, but with a promise had,
May hold a man when even Allah's word
Hath spent its force with him. Now, good my lord,
In going ponder this: The world is old,
And there were loves and lovers ere thou camest.'

OTHMAN RENEWS HIS PRAYER FOR MALKATOON

"The daylight, gray along the cavern floor,
Went out on Othman, yet, with upraised face,
He prayed—'O Allah! To a moon's scant breadth
The sky is shrunk; for I am in a well,
And darkness, cold as water, covers me
Still sinking. *Amin!* Thou didst dig the deeps,
Or else there were no heights; and I will find
Thee at the bottom.'

"Then a lightning flashed
Within his mind, that he alone might see
The answer Allah made—A woman dead,
And in her grave, but oh! so beautiful,
And so like Malkatoon! Her hair as dark,
Her face as oval, with a brow as white,
And even in its childishness her form
The very same! And he began to shake
With mighty madnesses of word and act,
Thinking it was indeed his love he saw
There lying lost to him; but he was saved
From them; for it is as the saintly say,
They to whom Heaven kindly sends a light
Not only see but understand as well.
And he was glad, and shouted so the birds
Nest-keeping in the leafage of the door
Affrighted sprang to wing, and Darkness leaped
Into the grave and bore away the ghost—
So loud he cried, 'O Dervish, peace to thee!

And all the charmed sweetnesses of peace
To thine! Be Allah praised, for He but now
Laid bare the narrow room where, as in life,
And wanting only breath to be alive,
The woman sleeps who holds thee promise-bound;
And while I looked at her, I heard thee say
Again, The world is old, and there were loves
And lovers ere I came. And then I knew
Thy meaning. (Ah, never was selfish youth
So gently chidden!) And now, clothéd all
In patience, and with my hand in the hand
Of Faith, I go.'

VII

OTHMAN AND HIS TRIBE

" And home again, from good
Sheik Ertoghrul our Othman had a gift
Of hill-lands rich with groves of terebinth,
And brooks which, flitting down by tangled glades,
And babbling over beds of marble float,
Did often pause in open pools to mock
The skies above with bluer skies below.
And there in one dowar, most like a town
Of many brown-black tents, he drew his Tribe,
That they might learn how pleasant are the ways
Of peace, and that an hundred spears may gain,
And safely keep, what ten were sure to lose.

"And next he built a Mosque of unhewn stone,
But with a tall and stately minaret;
Then with the help of holy men he taught
His children of the Wilderness the creed—
Allah-il-Allah—simple to the ear,
Yet deep in meaning—deeper than the earth
Hangs swinging 'neath the amethystine floor

Of Paradise. And shortly they could give
The *Fah-hat*, word and *rik-rath*, and salute
With hand on brow and breast; then in their midst
He pitched two greater tents.

"'For whom are these?'
The tribesmen asked.

"'This one is for the poor;
And comes a stranger hungry, or pursued
By night or enemies, it is for him.
This other'—and his voice sank low and shook
With sudden eagerness—'is Malkatoon's.'

"'And who is Malkatoon?'

"'A benison
Withheld by Allah until my trial day
Is done—a Spirit out of Paradise—
And this way comes an Angel leading her,
For in the distance I have heard him cry,
Be ready.'"

Here the high Sultana paused
To closer clasp and kiss the little lord
Upon her breast for pride, and then again
For love o'erbrimming. "Oh, my Máhommed!
'Tis love that makes the bread and pours the wine,
And is in turn the bread and wine for love."

The words were dark, and yet, as morning falls
On struggling mist, the look she gave him saved
The meaning of the thought. Then, to the tale
Returning, she, "And so the Tribe was cared
For by the Sheik, with everything of theirs,
The winged and hoofed, the speaking and the dumb;
The dogs had meat, the cattle pasturage;
Even the camels shed their foxen shag,
And ere long rounded into comeliness
Of health and strength. And when at last
There was no charity or duty more
To others owing, he arose, and up
To Allah's gate despatched his patient soul
In *ihram* white and seamless, there to sit,
And watch and pray the breaking of the sign
The Dervish asked of him.

VIII

OTHMAN AND THE LORD OF ESKISCHEER

       " And Othman had
A bosom friend, the Lord of Eskischeer,
Youthful and warm of fancy, like himself;
And him he one day told of Malkatoon,
And of her sire ascetic in the cave
Above the spring; and of the spring he spake,
A wayside comforter of suffering men,
With endless cheer of draught and song and dance,
Lest that way they should pass, and scoffing say,
It is not true that God is everywhere.
And then he told of how he came to see
The wondrous child, and paused to bless the chance—
A favor shaken from the Prophet's sleeve!
And since that hour, he said, the beautiful
Apparent in the other fairest things
Was not for him. Nay, looked he in the sky
At night, the utmost splendor of the stars
Was all a-rust.

      " 'And is she then so fair?'
The listener asked.

OTHMAN AND THE LORD OF ESKISCHEER

"'I know not in the world,'
Our Othman said, 'by which to make thee know
How fair she is, surpassing all her kind—
Nothing of perfume to the nostrils sweet,
Nothing lovely to the eye, or to ear,
Nothing of music.'

"Thereupon they gave
Each other hand, and went their several ways:
Othman, a lover with his love in love,
And doing childish things, as if the air
Were not alive with elves to laugh at him;
Now grumbling to his horse of Malkatoon;
Now whipping quatrains rude and cradleish
Until they sung of her as heroine;
Or when a breeze came stepping o'er the grass,
Lusty with life, and promising to go
A distance, with finger or his sword
Upon the sluggish air he wrote her name,
And bade the breeze, 'Ho! slave of Solomon!
Take thou this writing to my Malkatoon,
Nor say thou canst not find her. In a cave
Scarce two hours hence by measure of my steed
In easy gait, a daughter's part she doth
By old Edebali, the Dervish saint
Well known alike to kings and common men.
Below the cave, and in its shade at noon,
There is a spring, the mother of a pool

Of lucent water. There I saw her first,
And there with equal fortune it may be
That, hasting, thou shalt find her; and if so—
O happy breeze!—be careful not to give
Her fright by any rudeness, but approach
Her gently—gently—would 'twere mine to teach
Thee by example! Fingers of the air
Should have a tender touch; therefore I yield
Thee leave to lift her hair—'tis black as night—
And bare her brow, and blow upon her eyes
A breath not strong enough to more than cool
The dewy lids; or thou mayst fluff her hair,
And with it whip the whiteness of her neck,
So thou disturb her not; for it may be
She dreams of me. Begone!'

                    " Thus Othman went,
Never a man so with his love in love.
Far otherwise the Lord of Eskischeer!
The reins hung low upon his courser's neck,
And nigh asleep, it drowsed and drowsed along,
While he, forgetful of his armèd heels,
And of his journey, and the mine of things
About him and above, in grim debate,
But silent rode, his mien that of one
Just stumbled upon a wonder of the world
Within him, half a feeling, half a thought,
A fancy formless, faint, a vague desire

OTHMAN AND THE LORD OF ESKISCHEER

At first without an object, and so strange
He could but question it. So on a waste
Of waters from the bursting of a wave
There springs a spray so pale and thin it seems
To mock the searching eye; and so as clouds
That ere long mantle Heaven, and possess
It utterly, are first but pallid mist
Of breaking waves, the small desire became
A passion with the Lord of Eskischeer.
And on a hill-top, looking back, he stopt
At sight of Othman in the vale below,
And shook his hand at him, and said aloud:

"'Thou black-browed son of Islam, go thy way,
For 'tis the fool's, and thou becomest it,
A torch not more the night. Thou not to know
That every sense we have is but a gate,
An airy gate on downy hinges hung,
For Love to come and go! Keep the way; pave
It end to end with fantasies in rhyme,
And dreams of Allah, and Edebali,
And Malkatoon, and, with thy comrade fools,
Chatter and sing, and plague the fainting sky
With beat of drums and flaunt of flags; nor leave
Behind the combings of the Wilderness
Thou callest thy Tribe. And I will to the cave;
And should the Dervish give the girl to me,
Vex not the sun or moon or tender stars

With antics of a child. I had not loved
Her but for thee.'

"Then to the cave he sped
With might of galloping.

"A thousand knights
In gold-gilt steel, and girt with belts of gold,
And trebly proud of azure blades, new moons
In curvature, and casting brightness far
As stars ablaze in cold Caucasian skies,
Held all the space about the beaten road
Uptrending to the leafy door; their tents
Enwhitened linen circling one of silk
Capacious as a field, and dyed in green
And purple, graceful as a peacock's neck,
And full as iridescent; and the air
Above the camp was glorified with flags
And bannerets, one richer than the rest,
And heavy with symbolic broidery,
Bespeaking old Iran. Yet, passion-mad,
The Lord of Eskischeer thrust through the maze
Of martial splendor.

IX

EDEBALI AND THE LORD OF ESKISCHEER

"'Art thou he men call
Edebali the Dervish?'

"'I am he,'
The sage replied.

"'Thou hast a maid of age
To marry, and indeed they call her good
And beautiful.'

"The Dervish knit his brows
Till in the sudden gloom his eyes became
Like blossom coals of fire.

"'Now, who art thou?'
He asked.

"'I am thy neighbor—Eskischeer,
My castle, turreting upon a hill
Of wide espial, and a town with gates

Many as thou hast fingers on thy hands.
My hall hath space to dine five hundred guests,
And bring they horses, each may have a stall.
And for this cave I offer her a roof,
And safety well assured by mangonels,
And arbalists, and cranes, and bows of steel,
And trained men breastplated, and myself,
By no means least of them.'

       " The Dervish put
A bit upon his soul.

      "' But thou art Greek,
While she was born the daughter of a Tribe.'

"' She shall forget the Tribe.'

       "' Can we forget
So easily, my lord?'

      "' A woman can.'

"' Then what of holy Faith? Thou holdest Christ,
While she '—

    "' Nay, Dervish, jesters I have known,
But never one with face so gray as thine.
Or if thou must amuse thyself with me,

Be it, I pray, with something serious—
A ribbon, bright or dull, which I can skein
About my finger, or a flower of spring,
Which stales at noon of plucking in the morn—
For they are solid things compared with faith
In women.'

        " Then the Dervish meekly said,
His soul in curbing yet, ' In Paradise,
O good my lord, when all was dewy fresh
And garden-like, the Maker—be His name
A prayer forever!—with the first man walked
Familiarly, and from a mountain bade
Him view the world, and asked, " How seemeth it?"
And the man, then of nature firmly fixed,
Took time to answer. "Lord," at length he said,
" I see a wondrous glistering below
The daisies and the grass."

          "'The Maker's brow
Lost half its halo, and in the falling robbed
The wide-spread scene of more than half its light;
But with His awful glance askant, He said,
"The first is gold; the next thou seest is white,
And it is silver."

         "'And the man's eyes flashed
With covetous delight. "And are they mine?"
He asked, in heedlessness of selfish greed.

"'And slowly he had answer: "They are thine;
I made them, and the world, and everything
In sight beneath the welkin's bending arch
For thee and thine."

"'And still the creature stood
Fast-holden by the glisters visible
Below the daisies. Then the Lord was stirred
With jealousy. "Thou fool!" and down the height
The deep voice rolled, and smote the smiling vales,
And shook them as with thunder. "Turnest thou
From Me to them so soon?"

"'And then the man,
Remorseful, washed his face in dust, and cried,
"I will not other God than Thee—I swear!"

"'"I thought to win thy faith"—thus spake the Lord;
"Thou hast not other pledge to give for love
And worship."

"'But the wretch's grovelling,
And tears, and prayers, and promises prevailed
Upon the Maker. "Ask Me not to trust
Thee ever. Yet"—and in the pause His voice
From fiercest chiding passed to tenderness—
"The earth shall praise Me for its loveliness;
And that it have a tongue in lieu of thine,

O ingrate! I upon thy throne will seat
A woman to divide the power with thee,
And in her being, in the galleries
Of her heart, I will hang my lamps of faith,
And keep them burning. Or should Darkness blow
Them out, all this so passing fair to sight,
The beauty and perfections, and the gold
And silver thou hast taken for thy gods,
Shall crumble, and to nothingness return.
Amin!"'

"With that the Dervish, all uprist,
And towering, in the instant flung his mask
Of meekness off. 'Reviler thou of God
And woman! Get thee hence,' he said, 'and try
Repentance. Though in riches thou surpass
Kàroon,' my Malkatoon 'gainst thee shall bide
In sweet reserve, a pledge of love and peace
From Allah.'

"And he gave the Greek his back,
And left him dumb-struck.

---

¹ The story of Kàroon is given in the Kur-án. He is represented as the most beautiful of the Israelites who went out with Moses; and "Rich as Kàroon" became a proverb.

X

THE LORD OF ESKISCHEER IN QUEST OF OTHMAN

                " Then when brooding night
Was fallen, and the air so drenched with rain
Of darkness that a mousing fox had lost
His homeward way, Edebali forsook
The friendly cavern, and with Malkatoon,
And all his houseling and priceless store
Of gifts and honors, fled to Ertoghrul,
The thousand Persian knights in snowy tents
Encamped before his door at set of sun
Escorting him. The famous Sheik received
The saintly guest with rites by custom long
Prescribed, and in an ample plane-tree grove
He pitched for him a tent but lately loomed
Of clippings from his brown-black flock, more worth
Indeed than royal robes. 'Dervish'—thus the Sheik,
While making offer of the leben-draught
In shadow of the woven door—'a cup
Of welcome! Drink, and dread naught.'

                          " Homeward rode

THE LORD OF ESKISCHEER IN QUEST OF OTHMAN

The Lord of Eskischeer to nurse his hate
Of Othman. Fifty lances, with their steeds
Accoutred, kept he bedded in the stalls
Beneath his banquet-hall; while through the nights
The iron baskets of the linkmen flamed,
And filled the portal's hollow arch with light,
So if now or then a courier came
Fast riding, and with news, 'To saddle, all!
Sheik Othman is abroad!' one bugle note
Would mount the troop, and down the bridge would go,
And flying hoofs in tumult pass the moat,
Rolling and rumbling drumlike, but with thrice
The thunder.

"Chance as often favors wrong
As right. Another dweller in a house
Well castellated—Inæne by name—
To Othman sent a message: 'Come, I pray,
And be my guest!' And so it came to pass
That Othman and his brother, Goundonloup,
Were two of many friends, from near and far,
Assembled by the Lord of Inæne
To test his cheer and hospitality.
And wine and meat within the walls were free
As sun and air without, and every mood
And habit had its pastime day and night—
Chess for the old, and for the robust games
With coloring of royal war.

"One day
The sport swelled loud at table—loud the jest,
And louder yet the laugh—when from the gate
A guard appeared. 'My lord, a company
Of strangers stand before the barbican.
The chief invites the Lord of Inæne
To parley there.' 'The chief? Gave he his name?'
'He called himself a friend, and gave his name,
The Lord of Eskischeer. And with him ride
A soldier, Michael of the Peaked Beard,
And fifty pennoned lances.' The host arose.
'I know this errant lord, a man of note
And courtesy. Come, let us to the gate.'
And they arose, Othman and Goundonloup,
And all the noble guests in festal garbs,
And went with him; and on the battlement
Above the barbican, secure behind
The massive merlons, they stood and heard
The parley. And the Lord of Inæne
Was first to speak. 'Lo, here am I,' he said.
Then he of Eskischeer: 'Take thou salute,
And since in blood and faith thou art a Greek,
I bring thee chance to prove how much thou lov'st
The Virgin Mother, and her Sinless Son,
The Only Resurrected. Unaware
Thou dost high Christian honors render one
Who Pagan prophets proudly say was born
To undo Christ and Holy Church, and give

THE LORD OF ESKISCHEER IN QUEST OF OTHMAN

The East, and all of us, and all we have,
To Islam.'

    "Then the Lord of Inæne,
In wrath and 'mazement, 'Take thee hence, or name
The monster!' And the guests, their voices shrill
With passion—'Name him! Name him!' And the Lord
Of Eskischeer—'There!—see him at thy side—
Sheik Othman!—If a Sheik can be whose Tribe
Hath life from camel-eaters, altar-thieves,
And overflow of spawn from hatcheries
A-fester in the desert. I demand
Him of thee, and to scruple now were sin.
God-service his who cuts him off betimes.
Make haste, my lord.'

    "Then every eye was turned
To Othman, and he asked, 'My fellow-guests,
What faith have ye in trials by the sword?'
And they returned, 'The faith we have in God.'
To which he, smiling, as if more than pleased,
'So think I.' Then with changèd voice and brow,
And sternly, to the host—'Six tribesmen brought
I hither, newly mailed and horsed, and they,
And I, and this my brother—eight in all—
Will ride against the Lord of Eskischeer
And caitiff Michael of the Peaked Beard.'

    "The noble company, though belted knights,

THE WOOING OF MALKATOON

And often battle-tried, recast their looks,
Each mutely measuring the deed proposed
By other deeds in song and story long
Adjudged heroic; and in the while, a breath's
Brief space, from out a sea within their breasts,
Unknown to them, a wave of tenderness
Arose and thrilled them all—so young he seemed,
And in his high resolve so beautiful!
And into words they ran: 'It shall not be
If thou art lost, then is my honor lost,'
Thus the host; and another, 'Stay, and count
Their lances—fifty trained and merciless!'
But Othman answered, 'What have we to fear,
Who ride with Truth and Right?' And to his host
Again, and cheerily—'The parley keep
While we to horse, and when below thou seest
Me signal with my hand, then let there be
No toying at the gate, but fling it wide—
Both valves at once—and leave us to our swords,
And Allah.'

XI

THE COMBAT

        "Variant and loud and hot
The wordy strife the Lord of Inæne
Provoked and waged with him of Eskischeer;
As when two winds in mimicry of war
'Counter each other swirling round a house
Of many angles. Then, all eagerly,
That they might hear, the hirelings in the road
To shoulder swung their shields, and careless brake
Their fine array. And presently the gate
Opening moved—slowly first—noiselessly—
And then the hinges shrieked as if a ghost
In pain were giving up, and on the right
And left clang!—clang!—the sturdy, steel-bossed valves
Rolled swiftly back, uncurtaining an arch,
Shallow and tunnel-like, through which a glare
Of daylight from the thither side, snow-white
And blinding, smote the startled leaguerers.
Then, ere a man of them could frame a thought,
Or whisper of the treachery he feared,

THE WOOING OF MALKATOON

They heard a cry, 'Take, all, the stirrup now,
And follow me!' And in the voice there was
The ring and searching quality of calls
By trumpet wildly blown, which, when they find
A spirit, seem to say, 'Oh-ho! Awake!
For here is bloom of glory roseate,
And thine the gathering!'

"And wider grew
The stare of those in hire beneath the wall,
When through the gateway burst the beat of hoofs
Rumbling the earth as 'twere a slackened drum
By drunken drummers beaten. Motionless,
Their senses in a listless pause, they stared,
And waited what might come. So, when a cloud
Low overhead has clapped its mighty hands,
And, bidden halt, the startled traveller stands,
And bates his heart and breath, unknowing where,
If deadly bolt there be, the bolt may strike.
And then the meaning brake!

"Into a court,
House-bound and narrow, but aglow with light,
A horse appeared outstretched, and leaping long,
Its head low borne, its nostrils flashing red,
And straight upon the riven air back streamed
Its forelock, black, and plentiful, and long,
In freedom flying with the flying mane;

THE COMBAT

And on toward the open gate it ran,
Ringing the roughhewn flagging underfoot
As with their hammers anxious swordsmiths ring
The bladed steel fast chilling in the tongs.
And when the rider, all in linkèd mail,
And of the steed a part—so easily
He kept his seat—beheld the enemy,
He dropt the bridle-rein, and raised his shield
And scimitar full arm's-length up, and prayed,
'Shadow me now, O Allah!' Then to those
Behind him following close—Goundonloup
And the six tribesmen—half he turned his face,
And shouted, 'On, O brethren! This the way
To Paradise! Forward, and strike, and cry
"Allah, O Allah!"' Then frontward he set
His face all radiant with battle-light,
And shouting 'Allah! Allah!' as he bade
His men, into the vaulted gate he plunged,
And the great stones above him and below
Shook as he passed.

"And then a terror struck
The leaguerers, and every bridle-hand
'Gan tugging at the reins in selfish haste
To get away; whereat the guests in perch
Between the merlons, looking down at them,
Brake into gibes and laughter, and the host
Cried out, 'Oh-ho, my Lord of Eskischeer!

That infidel and traitor to the Truth
Ye asked of me—the Sheik without a Tribe—
Is coming—nay, is here!'

                       "And at the word,
As if it were some cabalistic sign,
Out of the hollow arch, then darkening
With turbaned friends fast trooping at his heels,
Blatant and eager—out into the hard
And trodden space before the portal front,
Our Othman rode. One buffet with his shield,
And Michael of the Peaked Beard went down,
Not slain, but sorely hurt, and tasting dust
In bloody mouthfuls, and all his wits awing,
As in some placid evening sky at play
With swallows.

                "Then the end rushed in apace.
From Michael to the Lord of Eskischeer
Sheik Othman wheeled Antar, and in the two,
The horse and man, there was so much of force,
So much of all a victim sees and hears
To stop the beating of his baser heart
What time the lion makes his flying leap,
The Greek turned sick with fear, and, borrowing
From panic, flung about, and fled amain.
And on his back, unwrit, yet plain as moon
In freshness burst above a scumbled hill,

THE COMBAT

The word that sent his hirelings down the road
They came, a scuffling, dizzened mass in blind
And headlong flight for life. Wherewith it seemed
The guests went mad with very ecstasy,
And merry-making set the stones they stood
Upon astir with laughter. But the voice
Of Othman through the din shore sharp and high,
'The *rakhem*¹ ruffling yonder—take thou these,
The sword-hands of my choice, and follow them;
The craven lord, their master, leave to me,'
Thus he to Goundonloup.

　　　　　　　　　"There was a path
By usage long and wearing won from sward
And broken place, and, like a rusted belt
Around a woman's waist, it girt the wall,
The blackened gate in lieu of silvern clasp—
A narrow way, and sinuous, and sown
With flinty fragments sharp and dangerous,
And never traversed save by sandaled men,
And kine, slow-footed, watchful—such the road
The Lord of Eskischeer in panic took,
And now was spurring down. And seeing him,
Again Sheik Othman in his stirrups rose,
And lifting sword and shield and shining face,
'Shadow me now, O Allah!' thus he prayed.
And bending low along his courser's neck,

¹ Vultures.

As spirit unto spirit speaking, said,
'Antar! Antar! O king of running kings!
Forget not now the soul thou hadst from me
The day we journeyed down to No Man's Land.
Forget not now the many other days
We gave to hunting lions, and in chase
Of eagles. Here, ignobler work—a wolf,
Only a wolf—but ours no less to give
The world a long, sweet rest by making end
Of him. So now, take thou the reins, and go
In freedom. Only bring me to his side,
And hold me there a time to strike a blow
For Malkatoon and holy love; and she
Shall feed thee from the palm-cup of her hands,
And comb thy mane, and braid thy forelock ply
And ply with night-black tresses of her own.
To thy wings, O Antar!'

" The reins dropt loose;
Then as a hound unleashed and bidden go
Leaps whimpering up with eyes afire to see
The game, and take direction from its flight,
So from a gallop, kept that it might hear
The master's promises—or so it seemed—
The willing courser tossed its shapely head
On high—a moment thus—then off it sped
In quickening leaps, of lions none so strong,
Of eagles none more swift; yet scarce less strong,

"OLDMAN IN HIS STIRRUPS ROSE"

UNIVERSITY OF
CALIFORNIA

THE COMBAT

And swift, and sure of foot the steed that bore
The craven Greek. Two boles of furbished steel,
In passage trailing light, like moving flames—
Such the men. Ledge-rocks wrenched from cloudy height,
And plunging down a graded mountain-side
In rivalry of ruin—such the steeds;
One bearing Love, and all its urgencies,
The other scourged by Fear, gray-faced and blind.
And answering the calls by Rumor passed
From court to hall and kitchen, noisily
And fast the castle poured its tenantry
Upon the wall, and from the vantage-points—
Embrasure, mullioned-port, and hanging-tower—
They viewed the race, in silent wonder first,
And then with gusts of clamor. '

                         "And thus once
Around and to the gate again! And scant
The time allowed the guests still waiting there
To speed their friend; for past the yawning arch,
And over Michael, writhing where he fell,
His senses yet abroad—on unseeing,
And hearing nothing save the steady roll
Of hoofs behind him—on into the path
The very same but then so hotly come,
The Lord of Eskischeer went thundering,
His shield-arm nerveless as an empty sleeve,
His sword forgotten. Like a flash he passed,

And then another flash, and Othman passed,
And still the reins hung loose, and still he talked
As to a boon companion. 'Not so fast,
O brave Antar!—I see his rowels drip—
And as our enemies the eagles used
When they would see if Jinn of Solomon's
It was pursuing them, a little stay
Thy wings, and hover—hover! There—now hold
The flight at that until I bid thee swoop—
And doubt her not—doubt not that she will feed
Thee with her dainty hands, and comb thy mane,
And braid thy forelock. Never amulet
Of pearl in lucent bar from Persian sea
Thrice laid upon the Kaabah's sacred stone
So blessed and blessing as a tress of hers!'
And then there was a yellow cloud of dust,
And withered grass, and leaves, and blasted shreds
Of rue from out the wrinkles of the wall,
Awhirl and breaking into lesser clouds,
And thence a muffled pounding of the earth
In rapid strokes, as if an hundred hands
Were breaking sheaves of corn with iron flails;
And so from view of those above the gate
The racers vanished.

"On, nathless, they went—
On over levels, meagre, green, and scant—
On into shallow brookways then but beds

THE COMBAT

Of rattling shingles—on—and as they went
The air they tore through sounded in their ears
Like wanton winds in revelry with waves;
And all the shouts dropt ringing from the wall,
The taunting and the laughter, mixed with cheers,
Passed them unheard. But coming presently
To a long, upward slant of hardened road,
Bent sharply round an angle turreted
And next the gate, our Othman woke to life.
'I saw the quarry stagger—there—again!
The time is come! Drink now thy fill of air,
Antar, and, by thy Nejdee blood, set on,
And prove thyself!' And crying thus, he snatched
And shook the reins, and as a swimmer breasts
A foaming current, leant against the breeze.
No more of waiting! Forward—forward sprang
The gray-black king of coursers, free and fresh,
The morning's vigor in his lissome limbs,
And in his spacious breast a hero's heart;
And this the prayer he heard at every leap:
'Speed, speed, O gallant friend! For Prophet's grace,
And holy love, and honor, and the Tribe;
Stumble not now, nor tire.'

"Nor vain the prayer!
There where the road, its gentle rise complete,
Around the castle's corner wound itself
In broadened loop, returning to the gate,

THE WOOING OF MALKATOON

Sheik Othman had his wish, and by a thrust
Half given he could have reached his foeman's back,
And that way set his swooning spirit free.
But all his scorn of doubtful ruse and mean
Advantage rose betime. 'Show me thy front,
And up with shield!' So bugle-clear his voice,
And loud, they heard it on the turret's top;
Yet, save to deeper stab his failing barb
And closer cringe, the Lord of Eskischeer
Rode signless on. Then once, and silently,
Above the Nejdee's neck our Othman shook
The flying reins. A leap, and flank and flank,
Stirrup 'gainst stirrup, on the straining steeds
Like shallops lashed in waters rough and swift,
Together drave. 'That thou, O craven Greek!
So much the lower of thy high degree,
Didst dream or think of loving Malkatoon,
Or fancy Heaven had bred such rose to waste
Its perfume on thy breast, were scarlet shame
To innocence.' Thus Othman, speaking low;
And then aloud, and near the gate, 'Awake!
It is for life, if not for love. Thy sword
Is there, and here thy shield, and under eyes
We come.' Moved then the wretch's bloodless lips,
'For the dear Christ'—he stopt. And in upon
The naked space before the gate they burst
With beat and gride, and on the battlement
There was nor laugh nor cheer; for overhead

THE COMBAT

The sword of Othman fashioned coils of flame,
And hissed like angry serpents. And he said,
'False friend and coward—liar—this the fate
The sinless Christ reserves for all thy kind!
Amin!' A shriek responsive to the blade
In practised stroke—a clang of shield and sword,
And steel in loosened links—a lifeless bulk
Full length in dust—these held the guests in awe
And speechless, while the courser of the Greek
Ran on alone.

"Then Othman stayed to say,
'My Lord of Inæne, I pray thou have
A care of this one, Michael; he is hurt,
Not dead. I will return.' With that, he rode
Off after Goundonloup; and together,
As tireless huntsmen follow skulking wolves,
Up to the very bridge of Eskischeer
The eight their harry of the hirelings kept.
And loud the greeting when to Inæne
The victors drave the harvest of the fray—
Well harnessed horses, lances, swords, and shields
Enriched with many strange devices done
In gold and staring pigment, spurs of gold,
And armor silver-gilt. And of it all
The host with deftest art made pyramids,
And sheaves, and radiates, and glorified
The banquet hall."

　　　　　　　　And here, as was her wont,
The fair Sultana-mother, wise and good
As she was fair, allowed herself to rest
The brave recital, and observe the child,
And wonder at his wonder; then, her arms
About him, and with kiss, she pledged the world
Another Othman, and in softer tone
Renewed the tale.

XII

OTHMAN AND ISLAM

"It seemèd then that all
The things of farthest flight, the birds and winds,
The mornings, and the weird Invisibles
Of Night which, as Voices, direct the winds
In ministry to men by Allah loved,
Made minstrels of themselves, and went about
Through Islam, even to its border-lands,
Singing of Othman and his victory;
And there was never fame so sudden won,
Or name so easy on the trumpet's lip.
And he was great, and—to the common heart
No sweet its like in life—his greatness came
To him in youth, when fronds of green enwreathed
Become a brow as light becomes a star.
It is the homage of his fellow-men,
And not the crown, that makes a real king.
And such was Othman; yet a lover more
Than king was he.

"Then in the prime of spring,
The third since Othman saw his Malkatoon,

THE WOOING OF MALKATOON

A gentle child with fluffy night-black hair,
And brow and breast of sun-illumined snow,
And seeming of the bubbling runlet born,
Back to the cave the saintly Dervish went
Without an enemy to give him fear,
Or break his thought on holy things intent.
And thither Othman often followed him;
At times sky-blind from overwatch of hawk
And heron heavenward in the blue blaze
Of hottest noon; at other times to pace
The cavern floor, and bear the elder's hand
Upon his shoulder, listening while he talked
Familiarly of Allah, and His laws,
And what might be if men but heeded them;
And always, sooth to say, it was a hope,
Or flutter of a wish almost a hope,
Which lured him to the good man's vine-clad door,
That something haply come, though but a dream,
Or nightly incident of fateful stars,
Would erewhile close the dreary trial term
Imposed on him. And many times there were
In which he overstayed the shortening day;
And then the sage and reverend host would roll
A bale of lion skins upon the floor
For couch, and smile, and say good-night, and leave
Him pillowed in the Prophet's nursing hands.

"One summer night—'twas in the red-moon month

Of nightingales, and sweetest rivalry
Of rose and jasmine—Othman, all belate,
Upon the couch of trophies stretched his limbs;
And over him Edebali had said
The parting speech wherewith the day is done,
And sleep invited in, when Othman caught
The sage's robe, and held it by the hem,
And in the tone a weary santon begs
The rich for dole to help him on his way,
Besought him, 'Stay, and tell me—thou who hast
The recollections of its joys to soothe
The pangs of love in loss—thou who canst tell—
No other can—ah, when—when is this dure
Of winter on my love to pass?'

        "The look
The Dervish gave the eager supplicant
Was wavering and cloudy; yet he could
But stay and hear.

       "'Here, father, are thy beads,'
Thus Othman further. 'See how dull and blurred
The ambers are from counting! And the cord
Of sacred green which holds them to thy belt—
The gray Scherif of Mecca blessed it thrice,
Then sent it thee from holy Arafat—
How worn and thin it is, and like to break!
O Dervish, pity me! As is the cord,

THE WOOING OF MALKATOON

My hope is wearing out, and like the beads,
My days and hours. Ah, when shall I have done
With counting them?'

    " And lower, lower drooped
The listener's cowlèd head, and not from age
Or wing of spirit noiseless in the air
The tremor of the taper in his hand.
And Othman hurried.

    "' It was in the spring
I asked for Malkatoon. Before your door
The birds were making nests, and easing toil
With blithesome songs; yet thrice since then the world
Has summered—thrice, and never word or sign
From her to me. Was ever honest love
So starved as mine has been? A little speech—
Good-morning, or, May Allah comfort thee—
Enough to tell me I was known to her
As friend to friend, and that she wished me well,
My soul had magnified into a song
As soaring and divine as Genii sing
To Israfil across the bridgeless voids.
Stoop lower, Dervish—stoop, and take my hand,
And tell me—thou whose wisdom is a gift
By gracious Heaven—tell me how my love
Has lived through all the going of the years
Without caressment, smile, or glance of eyes

Awake and shooting flatteries as stars
Shoot radiance—without the pleasant sting
Of rosy fingers softly laid in palm
Outstretched—without the music of a voice
In promises of deeper soothe than sleep
Or any drug. O Dervish, wanting these,
The daily bread and spiced luxuries
Of common passion, why should not my love
Have died of cold neglect, and been erased
From memory, if not itself the sign
Of Allah's favor you so long have asked
Of me? Yet here it is—at thy feet laid
Low again.'

"Still the Dervish held his peace.

"'Art thou afraid? Or'—Othman's voice sank down
And trembled plaintively—'Or didst thou think
My love a childish whim to change or go
With cunning play of truce? There have been times
I stopt the vagrant winds that seemed in flight
To where she lay, and charged them, Take her this
Or that—some airy frill of loving thought
Uprisen from the moment's wish like spume
From gushing wine; and still, so weak the years
To reave the passion of its early pulse,
To-day while coming here I heard the hist
And whisper of a breeze which might have been

THE WOOING OF MALKATOON

From her to me, and straight, as king to slave,
I bade it, Stay, and give me that she sent
By thee, and as 'twas rudely malcontent,
I slave-like prayed it, Be thou merciful,
And tell me if ye heard her speak my name,
And sigh when speaking it, as if she longed
To have me near her.'

"Then Othman closer drew
The good man's hand, and said with urgent look,
And voice impatient, ' There was one who spake
Of mighty deeds reserved for me to do,
And long and far his walk had been in thought
Of life and death, and what must come to pass
For sake of peace 'mongst men, and I believed
In him, and did the things he bade me do,
Nor gave a care to what was said of me;
And of my faith in him there grew a hope
Which should have been my steadfast law of life.
And of that hope—how often I have laid
My sword across my knees, and in its depth
Of blue reflection, limpid as the sky
Above me, seen the glory of the East
From out its wane emerge, and heard my name
Go down the winds a lasting melody
Of bugles. Prophet—say, dost thou recall
The lordly words? Yet marvellous and true,
That hope is not at all, or if it lives,

'Tis as an echo, lifeless of itself.
A dream arose, and blew its splendors out,
And left it hiding placeless in the dark,
A servant bounden to the dream.'

         " Thereat
The taper waved, and outbrake all the face
Of him who held it, reddening in the light.
'What is the dream?' he asked.

        " Then Othman's face
To scarlet turned, and, 'neath the searching eye,
Flamed like a poppy blooming in a field
Of yellow corn. 'I pray thee, turn thy gaze,
And waste its burning in the darkness there;
For that thou seekest I am moved to give,'
Thus he with purest modesty. 'For grace
I called it dream; yet asks it naught from night,
Or sleep, or waking reverie of day;
And if it goes, it comes again the same
In kind and radiance. 'Tis not a dream,
But living thought by sweetest fancies fired,
And always forward-flying to the hour,
The happy hour, when I can go alone
To Malkatoon, and raise her bridal veil,
And kiss the maiden blushes from her brow
And childish cheeks. O Dervish—by thy beard,
And Allah lending ear!—that joyous time

Were more to me than any fame of sword
Or deftest rhyme.'

           "In lowlands, after rain
Has washed the copse and of the earth made reek,
And mists of fleecy whiteness rise in clouds,
And through the tangle slowly drive like sheep
Unshorn and browsing, one looks up and sees
The stars in dewy faintness shimmering,
As if they were aswim in ruffled light;
So to the young man shone the elder's eyes,
Tremulous in their fixedness, and dim
With tears half-risen. Then the elder knelt
Upon the shaggy couch, and put an arm
About the younger's neck, and in the dale
Between the brows he kissed him twice, and said,
With struggling voice, 'Commend thyself to Him,
The Merciful and most Compassionate,
And sleep forgetful of the world and life;
And if thou hast a dream, on waking call
Me, mindless of the hour, and I will come
To thee.' Therewith he left another kiss,
And rising, round him drew his robe of fur,
And disappeared.

           "And later, when the clock
Of planets in the spacious heavens marked
A moment early in the afternoon

Of night, the chambers of the cavern rang
With loud alarms: 'Awake—Edebali—
Awake, and come to me!' And presently,
With taper lit, and robed, his face aglow
With sharp expectancy, the holy man
Upon the pallet sate himself in front
Of Othman. 'Thou hast dreamed a dream,'
So simply he invited confidence.
And Othman, 'Nay, a Vision came to me—
It was a Vision, Dervish.' 'Be thy care
Never so awful!' Thus, with caution large,
The elder spake. 'And know, my son, how broad
And grave the difference. Our dreams we have
From Angels—seven good, and seven bad;
And as the Angels, so the dreams they bring.
But Visions are from Allah, and He keeps
Them for His prophets, and for other men
A little lower, and already passed
Within the saving circle of His love
And mercy—Now I will not break thy thread
Of speech again.'

XIII

OTHMAN HAS A VISION

          "And Othman took the sign,
And slowly said, 'Upon this rugged couch,
O Dervish, I was lying by thy side,
And sleep was on us both. And in the drown
Of senses, dim and purple-sweet, there came
A sexless Genius, winged, and all unclad,
Except with starlight streaming from its brow.
And standing by me tall as any palm,
And whiter than a marble minaret,
It shot delicious waking from its touch.
"Soul of this man," it said, "attend." And straight
My soul had eyes and ears beyond the strength
Of mortals.

          "'"Look now!" and I could but look.
And the gray vestments on thy breast began
To stir and break, and forth appeared a moon
Full orbed, and with a rich enamelling
That made its light a lustrous pleasantry.
And over us it hung in far suspense;
Then like a feathered atom in a lake

OTHMAN HAS A VISION

Of crystal air, so lightly down it sunk,
And in my bosom vanished. Then in sway
Of mute perplexity my spirit stood,
And to the Genius turned; whereat it smiled.
And said, "The moon is fairer than a star,
And so is Malkatoon. But look again!"
And fain I looked, and saw a seminal
Of brightest velvet-green begin to rise,
There where the moon went down. And kneeling low,
The Genius breathed upon the tender spray,
And joined its palms above it, and arose,
And the plant, still in hover of the palms,
And rising with them, grew to be a shrub,
And then a tree; wherewith the Genius left
It to itself. But staying not, it reached
Its branches out, and covered us with shade;
And still outspreading, soon in need of rest,
It leaned its mighty arms on Caucasus,
And Hæmus, Atlas, Taurus, brethren all
From eld unspeakable. Nor did it stop
When hoarsely bidden by the restless seas,
Or spare the upper cloudways of the sky;
And everywhere that horizons had been,
And raised their baseless walls, and overhung
Them with deceptive veils of frailest blue
And purple, there was naught but foliage
And oaken glory. And then miracle
On miracle! The Genius did but lift

Its open hand, and speak some simple word,
Lo this or that! and fast the marvels came,
As they were hawks, and it their falconer—
Scarce faster break the ocean's turquoise waves
At beckon of the wind upon the beach.
In air I heard a whir of beating wings,
And looking, lo! the tree was filled with birds,
And butterflies besprent the living sod.
I heard a thunder of the quaking earth,
As if the sea had found its hollow heart,
And looking, lo! the granite rocks beneath
The sacred tree were rent, and forth the Nile
Upburst, and after it the Euphrates,
The Tigris, and the Danube, and when each
Of them had won its way apart and down
The wrinkled world, a holy calm befell.
And while I wondering looked, the Genius spake,
"This is the hour by men to Allah given.
Why stand'st thou there?" And to my knees I sank,
Thence on my face, and from the dust my lips
Sang worshipfully, God alone is great—
There is no God but God! And with the last
Refrain the Genius smiled, and waved its hand;
Thereat the realms in umbrage of the tree,
Now more a gilding splendor than a shade,
Unrolled before me to the farthest marge.
And on the mountain sides I saw the flocks
To fatness feeding; on the seas, I saw

OTHMAN HAS A VISION

The galleys ride the jealous dolphins down,
And flash their dripping oars in merriment.
I saw the hills put on their castle-crowns,
And in the plains, and by the littorals,
The crowded cities hold their courtly fairs,
And royal-wise, like queens in vanity
Of state, make high display of obelisk
And pyramid, and humbler towers and mosques
In princely fusion blent. And on my knees,
And near afaint, I heard the Genius say,
"Lo, this last—Look up!" And I could but look.
And all the singing birds grew still as death,
Then took to wing; and hardly were they gone,
When every leaf alive upon the tree
Became a curved and flashing scimitar;
And swinging pendulous and free, each rang
The other, so it seemed to me the whole
Vast overarch of air and sky became
A golden bell confused by silver tongues
Innumerable. And while thus the land
Was music-swept as by a throbbing tide,
An angry wind from out the Orient
Rushed at the sounding cone of flaming blades,
And in a twinkling every point was turned
In one direction. Whither? And to what?
I could but look. And on the farther shore,
Beyond a summer sea, I saw a town
Of palaces, and in its midst a hill,

And on the hill a church, and on the church
A dome whose lines seemed all to parallel
The smiling sky, and on the dome, itself
Of gold, a cross with arms and tree of gold,
So tall and beautiful it blazed afar
In fervid opposition to the sun.
O Dervish, thine it is to marvel now!
I could but gaze, and covet what I saw;
And in a trice the cross upon the dome—
No hand appearing—vanished with a crash,
And in its place I saw a crescent stoop,
And plant itself in moonlike loveliness—
Whereat I woke.'

           "Thus Othman closed the tale,
And then, like doomed men who calmly wait
The ruthless bowman's string, with folded hands,
And breathless, bowed his head. And presently
The Dervish, risen, touched the jetty curls
With trembling fingers, saying, ' Thou hast had
A wondrous Vision, Son of Ertoghrul—
A Vision, not a dream. A sentinel,
The whitest winged of all the white-winged host
That keeps the azure arch of Paradise,
Beheld thy spirit in the sapphire waves
Of deepest sleep submerged, yet making moan,
And struggling, so their ever-silent flow
Was broken; and he took it in his arms,

OTHMAN HAS A VISION

And mounted to the pitch above the sky
Whence it might see the World of Things to Come,
Apart from Heaven. Wherefore all that passed
Before thee in the Vision shall come to pass
In very order as 'twas given thee
To see them. That thou leav'st undone
And wanting shall remain a heritage
Of labor for thy sons, and sons of theirs,
Till all is done. Look, Son of Ertoghrul!
Lift up thine eyes, and with me see the Sign
So long in prayer at last by Allah sent
To make us glad! And, lo! his Will in love,
And the one Right Way by the Prophet stretched
Before me, like a path of gold aglow;
And she, the mother of thy Malkatoon,
So young, so fair, so pure the very grave
Did borrow beauty from her life that was,
Must now release me of the promise made
To her that awful hour when Death was come
And pouring darkness in her wistful eyes,
Which yet he could not all put out or reave
Of loving light; and if the Way should dim,
Or lose itself, or any need of help
O'ertake me, she, sweet soul, will hear my call,
And even guide me with her cheery voice
In lieu of helping hand.'

      "And then again

THE WOOING OF MALKATOON

The Dervish kissed his guest with joy amazed
And stupefied; but in his open palm
He kissed him, saying, so the gray-faced walls
Brake into loud alarms of ecstasy,
'Young father of my Tribe! Lord! Lord! my Lord!'
And so the old man sware himself thenceforth
A tribesman of the Tribe. Then he arose,
And going, turned to say full pleasantly,
'When hence thou goest, be it to appoint
The wedding-day, and with the feast concern
Thyself, remembering to make it large
And kingly. Every destiny must have
Its morning, noon, and night.'"

COMMODUS
A Play

INTRODUCTION

The story of Maternus was told originally by *Herodian*.

De Quincey, Gibbon, and Crevier have each a version of the story.

De Quincey's is as follows:

"A slave of noble qualities and of magnificent person, having liberated himself from the degradations of bondage, determined to avenge his own wrongs by inflicting continual terror upon the town and neighborhood which had witnessed his humiliation. For this purpose he resorted to the woody recesses of the province (somewhere in the modern Transylvania), and attracting to his wild encampment as many fugitives as he could, by degrees he succeeded in forming and training a very formidable troop of freebooters. Partly from the energy of his own nature, and partly from the neglect and remissness of the provincial magistrates, the robber captain rose from less to more until he had formed a little army equal to the task of assaulting fortified cities. In this stage of his adventures he encountered and defeated several of the imperial officers commanding large detachments of troops, and at length grew of consequence sufficient to draw upon himself the Emperor's eye and the honor of his displeasure. In high wrath and disdain at the insult offered to his eagles by this fugitive slave, Commodus fulminated against him such an edict as left him no hope of much longer escaping with impunity.

"Public vengeance was now awakened; the imperial troops were marching from every quarter upon the same centre; and the slave became sensible that in a very short space of time he must be surrounded and destroyed. In this desperate situation he took a desperate resolution; he assembled his troops, laid before them his plan, concerted the various steps for carrying it into effect, and then dismissed them as independent wanderers. So ends the first chapter of the tale.

"The next opens in the passes of the Alps, whither, by various routes of seven or eight hundred miles in extent, these men had threaded their way in manifold disguises through the very midst of the Emperor's camps. According to this man's gigantic enterprise, in which the means were as audacious as the purposes, the conspirators were to rendezvous and first to recognize each other at the gates of Rome. From the Danube to the

Tiber did this band of robbers severally pursue their perilous routes through all the difficulties of the road and the jealousies of the military stations, sustained by the mere thirst of vengeance—vengeance against that mighty foe whom they knew only by his proclamation against themselves. Everything continued to prosper; the conspirators met under the walls of Rome; the final details were arranged; and those also would have prospered but for a trifling accident. The season was one of general carnival in Rome, and by the help of those disguises which the license of this festal time allowed the murderers were to have penetrated as maskers to the Emperor's retirement, when a casual word or two awoke the suspicions of a sentinel. One of the conspirators was arrested; under the terror and uncertainty of the moment he made much ampler discoveries than was expected of him; the other accomplices were secured, and Commodus was delivered from the uplifted daggers of those who had sought him by months of patient wanderings, pursued through all the depths of the Illyrian forests and the difficulties of the Alpine passes. It is not easy to find words commensurate to the energetic hardships of a slave who, by way of answer and reprisal to an edict which consigned him to persecution and death, determines to cross Europe in quest of its author, though no less a person than the master of the world, to seek him in the inner recesses of his capital city and private palace, and there to lodge a dagger in his heart, as the adequate reply to the imperial sentence of proscription against himself."—DE QUINCEY. *The Cæsars.*

Here is GIBBON's rendering of the story:

"Maternus, a private soldier, of a daring boldness above his station, collected these bands of robbers into a little army, set open the prisons, invited the slaves to assert their freedom, and plundered with impunity the rich and defenceless cities of Gaul and Spain. The governors of the provinces, who had long been the spectators, and perhaps the partners, of his depredations, were at length roused from their supine indolence by the threatening commands of the Emperor. Maternus found that he was encompassed, and foresaw that he must be overpowered. A great effort of despair was his last resource. He ordered his followers to disperse, to pass the Alps in small parties and various disguises, and to assemble at Rome during the licentious tumult of the festival of Cybele. To murder Commodus and to ascend the vacant throne was the ambition of no vulgar robber. His measures were so ably concerted that his concealed troops already filled the streets of Rome. The envy of an accomplice discovered and ruined this singular enterprise in a moment when it was ripe for execution."— GIBBON. *Decline and Fall of the Roman Empire*, Chapter IV.

INTRODUCTION

The following is from CREVIER:

"Maternus, a common soldier and deserter, but of a determined disposition to undertake anything, assembled at first some deserters like himself, with whom he carried on in Gaul the trade of a robber; their success brought them new associates; his gang increased gradually, and became at last an army. There was a necessity of making a regular war against them, and Niger, who afterwards disputed the empire with Severus, was employed to encounter so despicable an enemy, and he acquitted himself like a brave and able officer. Meanwhile Maternus, in spite of the losses he had suffered, augmented his forces so far as to form a design of killing Commodus, and to make himself Emperor in his room.

"He perceived that he could not succeed in such a design if he showed himself openly, and as his art was equal to his courage, he formed an admirable plan: he divided his troops, and ordered them to go into Italy and to Rome in small parties, and went there himself; his scheme was to avail himself of the Cybeline festival, which was celebrated at Rome with great pomp, and during which every one had the liberty of being disguised; he therefore resolved to take for himself and his followers the dress and armor of the Emperor's guards, to mix with them in a kind of solemn procession where Commodus was present, to come near his person, and to murder him.

INTRODUCTION

"The project contained nothing but what was very practicable; but some of those who first entered into it conceived a jealousy of their leader. They had hitherto considered themselves almost his equals, and could not think of making him their master; they discovered the plot. Maternus was seized, with a great number of his accomplices, and they were all punished with death."—CREVIER. *History of the Roman Emperors*, Book XXI.

PERSONS REPRESENTED

COMMODUS.
MATERNUS.
CLEANDER, Imperial Favorite.
ANTONINUS,
POMPEIANUS, } Senators.
BURRHUS,
BURBO, brother to Maternus, and Chief of Gladiators.
MARCUS, Lieutenant to Maternus.

CAPTAINS { 1, 2, 3, 4 } with Maternus.

COURTIERS { 1, 2, 3 } to Commodus.

CITIZENS { 1, 2, 3. }

CLERK, to Cleander.
Landlord.
Boy, son of Maternus.
MARCIA, Commodus's mistress.
CRISPINA, wife of Commodus.
FADILLA, sister of Commodus, debauched by him.
WIFE OF MATERNUS.
QUEEN OF BACCHANTES.
Bacchantes, women of Cyprus.
Citizens, Officers, Messenger, Children, Gladiators, Charioteers, Attendants on Crispina and Marcia, Servant, Guards.

First Day

ACT I

SCENE 1.—GERMANY. *A wood. Wife of* MATERNUS *spinning flax. Her children, a boy and a girl, playing near by.*

Enter MATERNUS.

MATERNUS. My little, little puss [*taking the girl in his arms*]—my kitten all the day at play—come play with me.

Enter a SOLDIER.

MATERNUS. Tidings?
SOLDIER. Niger has won, captain. Our forces fly before him to this our centre.
MATERNUS. Well?
SOLDIER. An army closes upon us from the north, another from the south, another from the east, and from the west one.
MATERNUS. What more?
SOLDIER. More I have not.
MATERNUS. Thanks, good friend, and get you to eat

and drink; then, as the captains come in, bid them to
council here at midnight. Go now.
    SOLDIER. By your grace, captain.
        [*Exit* SOLDIER. MATERNUS *puts the child down, and*
          walks absorbed in thought. WIFE *quits her work*
          and goes to him.
    WIFE. Last eve at set of sun a crow did come
And perch itself upon yon withered limb,
And croak and croak; and all the while it held
Me in its evil eye. The chill I felt
Is on me now.
    MATERNUS.   Take up the wheel, and put
It in the cave. You will not need it more.
                    [*The boy removes the wheel.*
    WIFE. Not need it more?
    MATERNUS.   Ay; said the soldier right,
Good wife, the legions will be here at dawn.
    WIFE. O holy gods!
    MATERNUS.   And all they find they'll take:
This rugged cave, our home; these little ones,
And me and you, and such as living yield
Them willing slaves. They come four armies strong,
Our best outnumbered by the least of theirs,
And fighting is to die. What we shall do
Must be decided soon; and when 'tis fixed,
The council over, look you then to hear
What Fate does grudging leave as crumbs to Hope.
Go now, good, good wife. I will walk the woods.

Some watchful god may pity take, and show
A way to triumph yet, and better hope.
> [*Singing heard in the distance.*

Hark!
WIFE. They come this way.
> [SINGERS *approach.*

Song

The world goes up, the world comes down;
   Hit or miss, win or lose,
Blow good or ill, sail ship or sink,
   Great Rome must have her dues.
Of land or river, sun or air,
   Or ocean's fleeting foams,
Or mould of earth, or brawn of men,
   Naught is that is not Rome's.
   Up with sail, cast away;
     Farewell home;
   With us dance, with us sing,
     On to Rome!
     On to Rome!

> [*The* SINGERS *come up clashing castanets, tambourines, and cymbals.*

QUEEN OF BACCHANTES (*to* MATERNUS). We are poor, very poor—give us something.

MATERNUS. Who are you?

QUEEN (*singing*).
   Up with sail, cast away;
     Farewell home;
   With us dance, with us sing,
     On to Rome!
     On to Rome!

MATERNUS (*aside*). *On to Rome!* Is not this from the gods to me?
  [*He turns away, but comes back and drops some coin in the tambourine.*
Woman, a thousand thanks, and good go with you!
QUEEN. The best with you!
  [*Exeunt* BACCHANTES, *singing On to Rome! After them* MATERNUS *and* WIFE.

SCENE 2.—ROME. *Reception-room in the Commodian Baths.* MARCIA *reclining upon a couch.* ATTENDANTS.

MARCIA.[1] The baths are ours! Out now with all the fans,
And pour the perfume on them—on the tips—
So, so! Now sweep them here and back again;
And I will doze, and dream of rustling airs,
And flocks of birds in leafy groves of nard
And cinnamon.   [ATTENDANTS *fan her.*

Enter CRISPINA, *with* ATTENDANTS. *She regards* MARCIA *haughtily.*

CRISPINA.   I thought to have the baths
Alone.
MARCIA. What pause is this? Quick, bring the jar—
The jar of oils! A wind some kitchen 'scaped
Has stolen in.

[1] MARCIA maintained herself in favor until the death of Commodus.

[*An* ATTENDANT *brings her a jar of perfume, which she uncorks and applies to her nose.*

      O most sweet precious gift
For saving life! [*She kisses the jar passionately.*
    And by it hangs a tale.

 ATTENDANT. A tale? Dear mistress, will it make a laugh,
Be good, and tell it us.
 MARCIA.   To-day for oil
Of roses I did ask my august love,
My Cæsar, who did smile, and pretty say,
*That to the herd! To sweet thy sweetnesses
I have the oil ambrosial, even that
Great Juno brews for selfish use in baths
Olympian. Crispina did she touch
It once would die.* Thereat, with pity moved,
And wonder-struck, and yet as one does ask
A question rather by the tone and look,
O, O! I said. Then he, with ready wit,
And shake of head, which, from its many curls,
Showered me thick with odors delicate
And nameless, said, *Perpol! Hath one a taint
Of body anywhere, she shall not touch
This unguent of the gods.*—What, good my lord,
Crispina? so I cried, in quick alarm.
And to his ruddy lips he made me bend
My ear, so all my blood awake did run
To hear him say, *Ay, ay, she hath a wart
Upon her neck*—

ATTENDANTS.   O, O! ye gods of Rome!
MARCIA. *And one upon her breast of quickening growth.*
          [*Her* ATTENDANTS *laugh immoderately.*
CRISPINA. Let us go. I will build a Bath and keep
The keys myself.
MARCIA.   Ye gods! *Crispina's Baths!*
The name above the door would make the house
Abhorred; but did she use it only once,
Then though the meltings of the last night's snow
Were there received in limpid rivulets,
And all sweet oils and barks and richest things
Consumable were fed the fires to load
The air about it with their luxury
Of fragrance, still the very dogs would pass
It mutinous, with quick imaginings
Of sickness in the moon. No, no, rest us!
The world has plagues enough.
CRISPINA.   Begone—and take
Thy vermin pack—and haste—or I will make
Report of this.
MARCIA.   Now would the world were mine!
ATTENDANT. And then, sweet mistress?
MARCIA.   Then to Cæsar went
This woman as she says, indeed 'twould be
A service so enriched by what I most
Do wish that I would coin the universe
And give it her, and shame to think how poor
The payment was.—Crispina, Cæsar's here;

And 'neath the litter's purple blinds we were
In coming lip to lip and cheek to cheek,
With sighs so even drawn the two were one—
Nor will he hence without me.
 CRISPINA.   Do but hear!
They are not words that she assails me with,
But drippings of an udder so with lies
Distent it milks itself.
 MARCIA (*to her* ATTENDANTS). There—ring the bell!
          [ATTENDANT *rings*.

Enter SERVANT.

 SERVANT. Your will, most noble ladies.
 MARCIA. Does the august Cæsar tarry yet?
 SERVANT. Cæsar dines, and takes his bath, the eighth
  to-day.
 MARCIA. When will he depart?
 SERVANT. When Marcia pleases—so he said.
 MARCIA. 'Tis excellent well. Look now that my bath
Be ready made—the basin inside smeared
With paste of jasmine—and the water warmed
Like noon in summer—then the trick I had
From Cæsar when in playful mood we swam
Together—thou know'st it—rain half and half
With amber wine. He says it gives the skin
The hue of ruddy pearls— [SERVANT *turns to go*.
       But stay—I thought
The earth did sudden stir.

SERVANT. The earth, said you?
MARCIA. I thought the sky did thunder too.
SERVANT. The sky?
MARCIA. There, there—begone! [*Exit* SERVANT.
Were I my Cæsar's wife,
And angry, as Crispina is, the deaf
And dumb in Rome should swear the ground did quake,
And thunder filled the sky.
  CRISPINA (*to her women*). Come, we will go.
[*To* MARCIA.] This baiting thou shalt rue.
[*Exeunt* CRISPINA *and her following.*
MARCIA. Ha, ha, my sweets!
The baths are ours. Let's thither while we can.
An angry woman never won a man.
[*Exeunt, with laughter.*

SCENE 3.—GERMANY. *The woods again.*

Enter MARCUS, *with* CAPTAINS.

1 CAPTAIN. I think it best to fly.
2 CAPTAIN. We've held this grove until 'tis home.
1 CAPTAIN. I would live for that we yet may do 'gainst Rome.
3 CAPTAIN. The job is up for us.
MARCUS. My friends, let's rest debate. We run to cross of words; and after all Maternus will tell us what to do.

"THIS BAITING THOU SHALT RUE."

4 CAPTAIN. And here he comes.
1 CAPTAIN. See how slowly. The weight upon his mind does stoop his shoulders.

Enter MATERNUS.

MATERNUS. How stands opinion, brethren?
MARCUS. One set votes
To stay and fight; another thinks it best
To fly while time allows.
MATERNUS. But neither thinks
To give us tamely up?
MARCUS. Neither.
MATERNUS. 'Tis well.
Staying is but a wanton waste of lives.
Give them to me instead.
1 CAPTAIN. They're yours as 'tis.
CAPTAINS. Ay, ay!
MATERNUS. And next to such as plead for flight.
Between the lines unnamed, because unknown,
And this old wood, so long our resting-place
And shelter, is there where to plant our hearths
And be at home again?
1 CAPTAIN. I had not thought
Of that.
MATERNUS. Do not the Roman eagles feed
On hapless men like us in every land
Both far and near?

1 CAPTAIN.   Enough—I stand convinced.
MATERNUS. Well, we will neither wait nor run away.
Go call your men, and bid them that they set
Out for Rome.
  CAPTAINS. Rome! Rome! Surely not for Rome!
  MATERNUS. I said for Rome. In twos and singly bid
Them start to-night, observing to the end
That every speaking thing they chance to meet
Will be an enemy; so shall they come
To Rome the day before Cybele's day,[1]
By law the *Nones of April*, when, alike
In privilege, the people gladsome roar
The archèd streets with splendid revelry.
  1 CAPTAIN. We know the day.
  MATERNUS.   Such then the time and place;
And you may look for me in wait for you
Impatient at the old Flaminian gate.
Remember it. My treasurer will give
You for the road; then, preparation done,
Adieux to mothers, wives, and little ones.
And be ye tender with their tenderness.
It is but small for us to leave behind
The sweet hopes sure in woman's trustful heart

---

[1] The *Hilaria of Cybele*, better known as the *Megalesia*, began on the Nones of April; that is to say, on the fifth day of that month.
  There is reason to believe that the modern *Carnival* had its origin in the celebration of the rites accorded to Cybele, who was the personification of the Earth, or, in mythological style, its goddess.—DWIGHT. *Classical Dictionary.*

To wait on promises of quick return—
Which here they must abide.
>   CAPTAINS. O say not here!
>   MATERNUS. Where else have they?
>   MARCUS. Then keep them, loving gods!
>   MATERNUS. And us, good Marcus, keep they us as well!
Now hands in pledge. Let each one come to me.
>   [*They give him their hands.*
My Marcus, you will stay. To all the rest
A happy meeting 'neath the walls of Rome.
>   [*Exeunt all but* MATERNUS *and* MARCUS. MATERNUS *draws a ring from his finger.*
>   MATERNUS. Marcus.
>   MARCUS. Captain.
>   MATERNUS. You are my lieutenant now.
>   [*He puts the ring on* MARCUS'S *finger.*
>   MARCUS. Most duteous.
>   MATERNUS. Observe—When comes the *Nones Of April*, I may be in heaven or hell;
Then were there none to take and carry on
In void of me, O 'twere pity to melt
The ribbèd hills to tears! Wherefore of what
Awaits in Rome a word. You—I—and ours,
Assembled there, in arms and uniforms
Pretorian,[1] as guards from duty freed

---

[1] *Arms Pretorian.* The Imperial body-guard was habitually detailed from the pretorian cohorts encamped near the city of Rome. Their equipments were superlatively splendid.

And jubilant, shall help the thousands pulse
The pious riot on, till comes an hour—
O joyous throb of time for us reserved!—
When to the palace we will turn aside,
And finding Cæsar, kill him on his throne.
 Marcus. Kill him—kill Cæsar!
 Maternus.   O, you are so dazed,
My Marcus, I could laugh did humor serve
The hour in place of grief. So I will wait
Upon your wits.   [*He walks.*
 Marcus.   Now, captain, have you more?
I am myself.
 Maternus. Then tell me, Commodus,
The monster, dead and heirless, who shall have
His crown and capital?
 Marcus.   Why, he who bids
The highest, I should say.
 Maternus.   No—who but he
With strongest hand first ready? Doubt not more—
'Tis settled—fixed; wherefore to look again
Upon the nestlings of our wedded love,
And those who brooded them, and long ere this,
While blazed the night star o'er the western wall
Of eve, did cluck them chirping under wing.

     Re-enter Captains.

 1 Captain. By your leave, Maternus. You gave us trust but now in pledgeless sort, and that we will

amend. [*To his comrades.*] Out swords! [*They draw their swords and lift them high.*] Swear—swear we all to keep the appointment true!

CAPTAINS. We swear!

1 CAPTAIN. So good speed, good chief! We now are yours to order bound.

CAPTAINS. Life or death—Maternus! Maternus!

[*Curtain falls.*

Second Day

ACT II

SCENE I.—ROME. *Chamber in the Imperial Palace.*
POMPEIANUS, BURRHUS, *and* ANTONINUS[1] *in waiting.*

ANTONINUS. My spirit burns! Gods, how the minutes stretch
Themselves to lingering hours in plague of such
As wait at great men's doors, and on their moods
Expectant hang!
  POMPEIANUS.   Remember we have come
To serve our country.
  BURRHUS.   Ay, and by the smart
Of insult learn what 'tis to have a hope
Of this our Cæsar.
  ANTONINUS.   'Tis to call and call
And not be heard—to wait till comes the noon,
And then the night, and not a mouse to look

---

[1] POMPEIANUS, a noble Roman Senator, who, with Pertinax, had been an especial friend to Aurelius, the father of Commodus.
ANTISTHEUS BURRHUS and ARRIUS ANTONINUS, Senators and relations of Commodus, the former a brother-in-law. They were men of excellent character.—CREVIER. *History of the Roman Emperors.*

At us askant, and running, flatter us—
Three men are here.

    BURRHUS.   Three Senators!

    ANTONINUS.   Enough
That we are men!

    POMPEIANUS.   Our Cæsar is so young.

    ANTONINUS. To stand and see the empire of the great
Of Rome a plaything in a madman's hand!

    BURRHUS. I hear them—they come!

    POMPEIANUS.   Let us stand aside.

[*The three draw aside. An interior door is opened. Flourish. Armed* GUARDS *enter. Next* CHARIOTEERS *and* GLADIATORS. *Lastly* COMMODUS, *in costume of a charioteer, crimson reins over his shoulder and around his body, and in his hand a whip with gilded stock and long lash.*

    COMMODUS.[1] The very snails to top of wall have climbed,

---

[1] COMMODUS. It is difficult to believe this man sane. The incidents following are collated from John Mill's translation of Crevier's *History of the Roman Emperors.* If we can suppose the question of Commodus's sanity referred to a jury, and such circumstances submitted as evidence, with all the light of modern intelligence upon the subject, there would not be much room for disagreement. Thus:

    He immersed himself in most shocking debaucheries. His sister (Fadilla) did not escape his unnatural passions.

    His appetite for blood showed itself early. He had a pleasure in killing victims with his own hands. He dressed himself for the purpose like an executioner. He fought with gladiators. In such combats he used a sharpened sword, while they had nothing but foils with leaden points.

And cast their shells since work on it began—
Thy shoulder—lower stoop—up now—now hold
You there at that.
  [*He rests his hand familiarly on the man.*
        You saw it, said you not?
CHARIOTEER. As I see you, my Cæsar, quite as plain

During the administration of Perennis, his first favorite, he shut himself up in his palace, dividing his time between debaucheries and combats with gladiators and beasts. He killed four sea-horses at once, two elephants in two days, and a rhinoceros and a giraffe. By such exploits he fancied himself the rival of Hercules and Cæsar.

Actors of farces and obscene pantomimes governed him, while his hatred of the virtuous friends of his own father carried him to the point of murder several times repeated.

He buried the children of Avidius Cassius alive.

In his murders, when he wanted to prevent too great noise, he employed poisons.

He condemned to the beasts those who were witty against him. To this punishment he sent a party for reading Suetonius's *Life of Caligula*.

If he knew any one who declared he was weary of life, he took him at his word, and threw him down a precipice.

He diverted himself cutting off with a razor the noses and ears of his household, whom he obliged to sit down as if he intended to shave them.

He affected the surgeon, and, pretending to let blood, slashed the arms, and bled his victims to death.

He assumed to be a rival of Hercules, and, like that hero and demi-god, he fought with giants and monsters. For this, on one occasion, he assembled all those in Rome who had lost the use of their legs, and caused them to be wrapt up with cloths and linens below the knees, and of such length as to make them resemble the tails of dragons. He gave them sponges, instead of stones, for arms; then rushing upon them, he killed them with a club.

He had a passion for making a show of himself, driving chariots as well as fighting gladiators and beasts.

He passed much time in schools with gladiators, appeared with them

COMMODUS

I saw it past me borne, and set upon
Your stadium floor tenderly, as it were
Most fragile crystal which the lightest breath
Might stain incurably.
COMMODUS.   O beautiful!
CHARIOTEER. Yes, Cæsar, that thou art to common men,

in the arena as a professional; fought, and required the applause of the people and Senate. The gravest Senators had no choice but to applaud. He exacted his salary as a gladiator, charging a higher price.

Every time he did anything mean or cruel, or acted as a gladiator or master of a debauch, he had it registered in the journals of the city.

He fought three hundred and sixty-five times while his father was alive, and six hundred and thirty-five times afterwards: and so he gained one thousand victories—such as they were.

Nero raised a colossus for himself, which Vespasian afterwards consecrated to the sun. This Commodus appropriated by taking off its head and putting his own in its place. On the base he ordered the inscription, *Conqueror of a Thousand Gladiators.*

He devoted himself to Isis, and celebrated rites with the priests. Like them, he shaved his head. He helped to carry the image of Anubis. In the ceremony he struck the litter which supported the statue, so that the mouth and teeth of the god-dog knocked the ministers on their shaven heads.

He taxed the wives and children of Roman Senators two pieces of gold per head.

Once, wanting money, he feigned to go to Africa; obtained large sums for the purpose, and spent them in a debauch, pretending the people of Rome could not spare him.

Before the door of the Senate he set up a statue in a threatening attitude, holding a bow bent and pointed at the Senate.

He frequently showed himself in the dress of a woman.

He took his meals in the bath, and frequently took the bath as often as eight times a day.

He was the most consummate archer of his time, and withal the most beautiful man.

COMMODUS

It is to all the other chariots,
Sole incomparable.
    Commodus.   Ah, had you seen
The workman's face the time I bade him build
It so and so! His eyes did grow and stare
At me unwinking, round as moons at full.
                      [*He laughs loudly.*
    Charioteer (*to a* Gladiator). The world ne'er saw a
      Cæsar like to this.
    Gladiator. A Cæsar? He's a god!
    Commodus.   *My Chariot*
Must pay the sun in kind, and burn the eyes
Of them that look at it—so I began;
And when I saw I had him mind intent,
I further said: *Make you the yoke of steel,*
And all the rings of steel; the pole of oak
Without a crook or gnarl; and arm you well
The axle's ends with tigers' heads in brass,
The jaws gaped wide to snatch a living prey,
The eyes of yellow amber, all so wrought
That smith and sculptor may not carry art
Beyond them. Have you that? I stopped to ask,
And at his yes went on: *I want the spokes*
Of silver set as furbished radiates
In silver naves; the fellies ivory,
Tinted like cream from last night's milk of mares,
And tired in doubly tempered hoops of bronze;
The bed of willow leafed with lustrous gold,

COMMODUS

A twin of that the proud Germanicus
Did drive along the lusty triumph's way—
But hold! The ancients there?—
    CHARIOTEER.   We found them here.
    COMMODUS. They used to help my father kill his hours,
Mumbling of morals, and philosophies,
And other sickly mists of moon-struck minds;
And often, 'mid delivery, o'ercome
And spent, they sitting slept, and slept again,
And nodded in their sleep, as if the speech
Would of itself from wise to wisest run
Forever on.
    POMPEIANUS (*advancing*). O Cæsar, at thy feet
I lay an old man's love.
                        [*He kneels to* COMMODUS.
    COMMODUS.   An old man's love!
There let it lie—or better, do thou take
And put it in some deep and grewsome vault
Where worms have had their mastery, and been
In turn resolved to dust. I'll none of such
Companionship; for see you [*laughing*], did I want
A simple from the spiceries by all
The gods prescribed for dulness—dice, sword-play,
Or music, dance, or women—then to keep
My conscience in a prickly-heat, 'twould dose
Me with philosophy and apothegm—
And when a laugh were good, 'twould put me off
With husky groans. Go bring some lighter curse!

There's naught so damned as *No* when I would *Yes*.
Only the gods shall say me, *Well done this!*
Or *O alack for that!*
  [*He strikes* POMPEIANUS *with his whip.* POMPEIANUS
    covers his head, and BURRHUS *and* ANTONINUS *rush
    to them.*
ANTONINUS.   Hold, hold, my lord!
His every hair a silver trumpet is
To help the shrinking heavens plead for him!
COMMODUS. Make way—room—room, I say!
              [*He casts the whip-lash loose.*
ANTONINUS.   These war-worn hands
I lift protesting, not for self—a thing
Henceforth incapable except to stir
Of some, their sneers, of others, tears, as are
The men I meet—no, Cæsar, not for self,
But country! Send and take account of those
Who last night died of famine in our Rome.
And in your following—these ready thieves,
Whose presence here makes all earth else rejoice
Because they are not there—if one there be
To feel a stranger's woes, the plague[1] invites
Him to the western gates to see how fat

---

[1] Under Commodus, Rome was dreadfully ravaged by famine, plague, and extensive fires. The famine did not result from barrenness of the earth, but the wickedness of men. The plague was most violent in the city. The daily mortality averaged two thousand cases. Even beasts suffered from the contagion.

It feeds on Latin folk. But pity them,
And I—O Cæsar, I will kiss the hand
With which you aim to lash my honor out.
To mountains turned, the times do fall upon
And bury us.

  Commodus.   How often have you seen
Me sting an elephant until he brought
His bulk to dust, and tearful roared *Enough!*
                    [*He draws to strike* Antoninus.

  Enter Marcia. *She catches* Commodus's *hand.*

  Commodus. Give up the hand!
  Marcia.   Not even Jove could mend
The act it then would do.
  Commodus.   Let go, I say!—
Or am I that which I did think myself?
  Marcia. I do not fear my lord when not himself.
  Commodus (*to the* Senators). It were a little thing in
    you to thank
This woman for your lives.
           [*He recovers the lash.* Pompeianus *rises.*
                    Now be there one
Who fears me not, then is the world not mine;
And I will not a part of it, though 'twere
The bigger part; nor more will I forego
The very least, for then there could not be
A whole to own.
           [*He has the lash all in hand.*

111

COMMODUS

                Now, woman, say again
You do not fear me.
  MARCIA.   When at last I came
To see my lord in changing moods, now kind,
Now terrible, he made me know his breast
Was not a fitting place for Fear to lay
Its ashy cheek.
    [*She takes the lash, drops the coils around her neck,
      and carries his hand to them at her throat.*
                Good my lord, was not this
The purpose which I saw behind your eyes?
  COMMODUS. Now, by the gods, a fair, white, slender
    neck!
  MARCIA. My lord is slow.
  COMMODUS.   A shepherd's pipe of straw
Were not more frail.
  MARCIA.   And yet my lord does wait?
  COMMODUS. The life hides shallow here—a bird of swift,
Elusive flight, so often vainly watched—
Perhaps more slow in woman than in man.
Against this waxen cage's veinèd bars
It beats its scarlet wings—I feel them strain
For liberty. A bodkin's point would do
To set it off—a turn of hand would do—
It tempts me—gods!
                  [*He pulls her upon her knees.*
  BURRHUS (*aside to* ANTONINUS). I ne'er saw murder writ
So plain on any face. Let us retire.

ANTONINUS (*aside*). No, no! For if her courage does
 but hold,
She'll make the end, not he; and should she win,
There's hope for Rome.
  BURRHUS.   Hope?
  ANTONINUS.   Ay.
  COMMODUS.   I wait for tears
To prove a common soul but briefly dressed
In bravery!
  ANTONINUS (*aside*). He changes countenance!
  COMMODUS (*to* MARCIA). Have you forgot the day I
 set my chief
Of guard and old Trebonius in chairs
To shave them? Ah, their necks were under hand;
Against my fingers beat the lives I craved
To know about. Ha, ha! A pretty jest!—
I cut their throats! And as the gaping wounds
Did vent their bloody jets, the wary ghosts
Slipped noiseless by, and joined the kindred air—
A jest to move the Sphinx!—But thou—thou dost
Not laugh!
  MARCIA.   What, good my lord, upon my knees?
  ANTONINUS (*aside*). Would she were wife in place of
 her he has!
  COMMODUS.   O pretty fool! I'll take the lash away—
Damned jewelry unfit for such a throat!—
                               [*He removes the lash.*
Take thou my hand.   [*He assists her to rise.*

COMMODUS

                    There, now! The vulgar see
Thee statured as thou wert. Their eyes are eyes
Of worms and mining moles. They know not what
It is to have a Cæsar lend a hand
To help them.
              [MARCIA *throws herself upon his breast.*
  MARCIA.   Dear my lord! The other gods
In benefaction keep afar in space!
  COMMODUS. Thou cunning, cunning witch!
  MARCIA.   Oh! were I that,
I then could tell my Cæsar of my love,
And have him measure it, and laugh at him;
For oft as found, its limits I would lift,
And set them out of reach of thought again.
  COMMODUS. There is a subtlety which here in Rome
Men look for in blind wastage of their lives,
Not knowing where to seek it. Mastery
Of king and state, they call it, under breath,
As if the mention out would reach the gods,
And shame them for their lesser sanctity.
Will they to me, the dolts, and ask of it,
I'll fillip them with, Blow your candles out,
And quit your courtier arts before the throne.
'Tis true the prince is there, and there the state
In him enfleshed, but not the rule of them—
The thing you seek. Beneath a woman's tongue—
Under the rose-leaf lining of her tongue,
To dripping steeped in honey-sweet of words,

"WHAT, GOOD MY LORD, UPON MY KNEES?"

UNIV. OF
CALIFORNIA

The subtlety its luresome lodging hath—
As I but now have found. Ha, ha! For wounds
To feeling, Marcia, give me good results,
And doctors unto doctors for their dues.
        [*He kisses her.*
A salve upon thy throat!—and on thy cheek!—
Nor blood except upon thy pursed lips,
To mark where Cæsar left his taste of love!
Go now—and I must go.
   [*Trumpets heard outside playing a march.*

   A CHARIOTEER *runs out and returns.*

 CHARIOTEER.   Her Majesty
Is passing by.
 COMMODUS. Crispina! Ill the time
For her to come, and with her music bray
My recollection. Marcia— [*He leads her aside.*
       Have a care
Of her. That thou art fair and wise and brave,
And she is neither, therefore watchful be
Thou all the more.
 MARCIA.   The qualities wherewith
My lord possesses me were basely used
In other part than his. For him, in my
Offence conjoint, I will not cease to care.
From Argus I will borrow sleepless eyes,
And plant them open where she daily walks,
And open groove them in her chamber doors.

COMMODUS. There, there — go now — good-bye, until
again!
[*To his train.*] Move on—I long to see the chariot.
> [*Exit train. He follows, but stops and holds his
> arms to her. She runs to him, receives his kiss,
> then stands gazing after him.*

BURRHUS. We have failed.
POMPEIANUS. Ay, again, and Rome is lost.
ANTONINUS. Not so. This Marcia is a Roman born,
And come what may, I'll dare a speech with her.
MARCIA. What others seek the bosom of the night
To meditate, he dares the sun to look
And see him do; and where he goes or comes
The greatnesses by Time avouchèd best
Inconstant fall away to sullen flames,
Knowing comparison will snuff them out—
The Senators!
ANTONINUS. Fair mistress—
MARCIA. Good my lords.
ANTONINUS. We said when now in Cæsar's face we saw
You stand, *She is a Roman.*
MARCIA. So I am.
ANTONINUS. There is a sick one here whom you should
know.
MARCIA. His name, my lords?
ANTONINUS. Our Rome.
MARCIA. I knew not such
A body could be sick.

ANTONINUS.   Indeed so sick
We cannot walk abroad but horrors come
And chase us home.
    MARCIA.   Be plain.
    ANTONINUS.   We cannot find
A street that is not overrun by herds
Of children clamorous as cast-off dogs;
And wives and daughters, whom we knew as bred
In honor, make public cry, and to gain
The crusts they moan for, shake their patchèd rags,
And of their persons offer show so pale
And meagre, 'tis not strange if Death refuse
To waste himself upon them. And of men,
The stays of state, there are no rich and poor—
The poor have sunk to poorest, while the rich
Have run away.
    MARCIA.   Does Cæsar know of this?
    BURRHUS. It was to tell it him we came to-day.
    ANTONINUS. Nor more, I swear, for Rome than Cæsar's
      self.
There is a man who sits in highest place,
A conjurer of mischiefs for the state—
    MARCIA. Cleander?[1]

---

[1] CLEANDER—a Phrygian by birth. He was sold as a slave in his own country, and brought to Rome to do the meanest offices.

In the palace he became the Emperor's slave, and was agreeable to Commodus, when a child, by a likeness in their dispositions. This beginning he cherished. After his father's death, Commodus gave him his free-

ANTONINUS. Oh! I see he's not unknown!
MARCIA. A wicked man, and base, and studious
In husbandry of profits foully got.
POMPEIANUS. Our cause is won!
ANTONINUS. Without the harbor stands
A fleet of ships from Egypt. Could they land,
The city would be gorged with bounteous store.
MARCIA. Why come they not?
ANTONINUS. Cleander knows, not we.
MARCIA. 'Tis past belief.
ANTONINUS. Sweet mistress, these are men
Unused to play; like me, they stooping lean
Against the winter winds of life.
POMPEIANUS. 'Tis true—

---

dom, and appointed him first chamberlain. He also gave him for wife his concubine *Demostratia*.

Cleander was of mean soul, and abused his power. He put everything to sale—places of Senators, command of armies, government of provinces and intendancies—for all which he was well paid. Merit and birth were of no account with him. To increase his gains, he multiplied offices, and named twenty-five Consuls in one year. He had no regard for laws or precedents. Money bought absolution for crimes and release from judgments, sometimes with additional dignities. No citizen was secure of life or fortune if he had a rich enemy. Condemnation to banishment, death, punishments of all kinds, confiscations, deprivation of burial, were subjects of barter, and nothing thought of but the price.

By his cruel and abominable traffic Cleander amassed immense wealth; and to secure his gains, he shared them with the Emperor's concubines, and even with the Emperor himself.

He was magnificent in the use of his riches. He built hot baths in Rome, which he called *Commodian Baths*.

For hungry eyes have in the distance seen
The tacking sails.
    MARCIA.   The purpose—give it me—
It hides behind the horror.
    ANTONINUS.   A most just
Demand. You know, fair friend, that nothing could
So well become him as humility;
But so has Fortune been a serving-girl
To his conceit, and by her favors swelled
It out of bounds, that now his eyes are blind
With rage for purple; nor will any robe
But Cæsar's fit him.
    MARCIA.   Oh, I see, I see!
The cockle gapes his hingèd shell with wish
To be leviathan!
    ANTONINUS.   And see the tool
The traitor holds in hand. By that it does,
A sullen mob betrays its bloody dreams:
It whittles knotted clubs; renews the points
Of rusted swords; brings forth old shields and tries
Them on its shrunken arms; draws bands to head,
And chooses chiefs, and into moulds of new
Design recasts the metal of its hate.
And dare you now to Cæsar say these things
Which we to you have said?
    MARCIA.   'Tis mighty stuff,
My lords, and will not much endure mistake.
Give me to think of it.

ANTONINUS. Ay, give it thought,
But cap the thinking with the instant deed.
Our duty done, good-day.
MARCIA. Most excellent
And noble men, good-day.
POMPEIANUS (*aside*). Would Cæsar were
As gracious! [*Exeunt* SENATORS.
MARCIA. If a mob there be in stew,
The blinds of night thrice dipped in Pluto's shades
Were not enough to hide it. To the streets!—
Then to Cleander!—Ah, he comes this way!
Ye wilful gods! That in such swinish flesh
Ambition could enthrone itself! Behold! [*Exit.*

Enter CLEANDER.

CLEANDER. I am not longer minister of state,
But of my Cæsar's whims, which, day and night
More wantful, do but grow with surfeiting.—
Clerk, clerk!

Enter CLERK.

CLERK. Your will, my lord?
CLEANDER. Give me the list.
CLERK. My lord.
[CLERK *gives him a paper and retires a little.*
CLEANDER. This—'tis not the list—a lawyer's bond: yesterday he besought me to make him Prefect of Britain, and this his bond of payment for the office—need-

CLEANDER READS THE LETTER

UNIV. OF
CALIFORNIA

less now that I have his money. A goodly sum, by
Crœsus! My carps in pool, my calves and peacocks
in their pens, will keep their excellence on it until
they're dished — and Commodus is always hungry.—
Clerk!

CLERK (*approaching*). My lord.

CLEANDER. Not this, but the list I made last night
of the remaining rich in Rome.

CLERK. Pardon, my lord.

[CLERK *gives him another paper and retires again.*

CLEANDER. Grow I not old of body, if not mind,
Before I should in nature? Puffed of eyes?—
To wrinkles adding flesh?—My youth by aches
Of sixty filched? The fatted ox in stall
Has not a girth like mine, nor eats or drinks
He so to deadly fill; and in these hands
Unsteady palsy lurks with shortening term
To set them shaking at my doted will.
'Tis time to be a-doing.—Clerk, I say!

[CLERK *approaches and bows humbly.*
Yes, let us on—you first—but keep in call.

[*Exit* CLERK.
A little time to think—I've picked the bones
Of Labor white, and Trade, which had the art
Before my time of sending men in search
Of profit boldly to the world's sharp edge,
And over it into the general
Undermost, whispers now, and fearful holds

Them empty-handed in their silent marts—
And here in list and table are the names
Of all the rich in Rome, with what they're worth.
      [*He runs over the list.*
Ships, houses, lands—Greek, Roman, African,
Egyptian, Jew—patrician, priest, and pleb—
To auction this one, exile that, and Death
To have a lion's share! And then the end
In bloody brief of Master Commodus!
Already in the bearded husk I hear
The ripening rattle of the golden grain.
I'll push his follies on in madder gait,
And speed my fortune.—Clerk, clerk!

    Re-enter CLERK.

CLERK.   Here, my lord.
CLEANDER. Go not too far.   [*Exit* CLERK.
    If rheums and baldness haste,
And odious fat and age in youth attack
My bones untimely—let them! By the gods,
Though come the worst—I'll be a Cæsar yet! [*Exit.*

SCENE 2.—*Road through a mountain pass.* MATERNUS
 discovered sitting upon a stone.

MATERNUS. Are these the hands to free the yokèd world?
These aching feet, coarse clad, and ploughing slow

And wearily so many leagues of dust,
Are they at last to climb great Cæsar's throne?
The thought does father impulse strong as hands
To push me on, and I must yield to it,   [*Rises.*
Nor think of rest until the deed is done;
And then the weak and wronged shall sit with me,
And eat and drink, and merrymake and go,
Singing a holiday for every one,
And plenty. Such the Cæsar I shall be!   [*Exit.*

Enter MATERNUS'S WIFE. BOY *drawing a hand-cart, with baby in it.* WIFE *pushing the cart.* WIFE *seats herself on the stone just vacated by* MATERNUS.

BOY. We are near him now.

WIFE. What will he say at seeing us? You know he bade us stay at home.

BOY. The baby here—let her hold her hands to him, the little fingers all alive with asking, you'll see him laugh and give us joy for joy.

WIFE. Ah me, ah me! I love him so! 'Tis love that drives me on.   [*Singing heard.* WIFE *rises.*

BOY. The dancing girls!—I know their song.
    [WIFE *resumes her seat.*

Enter BACCHANTES, *singing On to Rome.*

QUEEN. Softly!—children—and a woman!
    [BACCHANTES *surround the family.*
Good woman, are you tired?

Wife. Yes.

Queen. And hungry?

Wife. My little ones may be.

[*The* Bacchantes *uncover packs, and give the children bread.* Queen *kisses the baby.*

Queen. Eyes so heaven-blue we never see in Cyprus. [*To* Wife.] Where away?

Wife. To Rome.

Queen. What have you to do in Rome?—a woman without device or gift—your youth given o'er to babes —and all incapable of riot or debauch.

Wife. I'll find my husband there.

Queen. Oh! 'tis far to follow!

Wife. Far indeed. But what of that when once I've found him?

Queen. Then there is such thing as love?

A Bacchante. No, no! True love, as you will find, has gone to blue the sky and salt the sea.

Queen. 'Tis this woman's life.—Good mother, we too are bound to Rome. Make your journeys with us, and we will share with you, and give you help—all for love of your love.

Wife. I must travel slow.

Queen. Well, we will wait at times to see how you get on.

Wife. I have but thanks to give, and a tongue to pray the gods for you.

Queen. Then you would pay us rich in unaccus-

tomed coin.   For the time, mother, good-bye—and to the little one another kiss. [*She kisses the baby.*
Come—up, my island born! Sing for cheer, and let's away!
[*Exeunt* BACCHANTES, *singing their song.*
WIFE. Oh! my heart beats fast, and I am faint! If once the city swallows him, we may never, never see him more.—Come, my darlings, let us go.
[*As she goes out pushing the cart, the curtain drops.*

Third Day

ACT III

SCENE I.—ROME. *Corridor of the Imperial Palace.*

Enter COMMODUS *and* BURBO *from the stadium, both in full gladiatorial armor of the class swordsmen.* COMMODUS'S *helmet and shield carried each by a page.*

COMMODUS. I think the total of my victories,
When last we cast it up, did stand at odds.
But now—how stands it now?
    BURBO.   This makes the score
A thousand.
    COMMODUS. Even, Burbo—speak it fair—
An even thousand, of their schools the best,
And equal armed.
    BURBO.   O Cæsar—equal armed?
    COMMODUS. By Hercules! so does the theme enlarge
With happy thought that you, unroughing, shall
To gentle turn, and write.
    BURBO.   What! Burbo turn
A clerk, a girl-faced, cherry-painted clerk,
And hang him lazy, lean, and limp above

A table, there to meekly scribble one
Day out in order that the next may be
As meekly scribbled in?—exchange his shield
For tablets?—put a button on his sword,
And hide it in a closet, lest it fright
His fellow-clerks?—have no manlier trick
Than filing blunted pens to point again?—
Forego the triumph, and the sweet rewards
Of crown, and cheer of hands and voices dropped
Like thunderous music from the peopled sky?
Why that would be a cheat on her who 'layed
Her mother's pain at sight of me to cry,
Exulting, *Ha, ha, ha! The child's a man!*

 COMMODUS. But what a tale is here—
 BURBO.   A tale—what tale?
 COMMODUS. Why, how in equal combat I have slain
A thousand men. Great Hector did not half
As much.
 BURBO. Oh! Once I heard it said, does one
Begin a lie, his tongue the truckling used,
The doors of hell with knockings ring for him;
But does he worse—takes he a pen to write
A lie that it may live, why then of choice
He sits already on a devil's bench,
And plies a trade to suit his company.
The saying, Cæsar, had a power on me.
I heard it in my youth, and scornful left
The cunning of the scribe to holy men,

And weaklings some way shorn or cursed at birth.
The sword did please me best. I cannot write.

COMMODUS. Then is my skill a precious essence spilled
And wasted!

BURBO.   What, Cæsar, tears?

COMMODUS.   Oh, the charm
And sweetness which I found in mastery
Are not more!

BURBO.   Why, there are in Rome who trade
In writing.

COMMODUS. Dull and damned insensates they!
Or, if they wrote of me, 'twould be to dash
The ink with gall, or whisper in the palm,
Some other did it.

BURBO (*aside*).   Oh, a Cæsar this!
[*To* COMMODUS.] Let's end, and go our ways — I want
   my wine.

COMMODUS. Hold, Burbo!

BURBO.   Oh, then, I will write 'tis true
He killed a thousand men; he armored full,
While they had make-believes for fence of head,
And shields to give at touch, and swords mere laths
To likeness tinselled.

COMMODUS.   By the gods, you try
Me overmuch!

BURBO.   And then to sum the whole—
Of those thus slain, I'll say all died with grace
Except the Romans.

COMMODUS.   Oh!—now—that of us,
Whose holdings all are spoils of war on war?—
Look here—my private seal.
                    [*He takes a ring from his finger.*
                         It signifies
The world, and yet I'll stand it simply 'gainst
The sword you wear.
   BURBO.   In wager?
   COMMODUS.   Thou the judge,
And all conditions equal, if I fail
To prove a Roman dies with less of fear
Than other men from wheresoever drawn,
The seal is thine, to order what thou wilt.
   BURBO. The burden's on you.
   COMMODUS.   Oh, an easy thing
To one who rides the world with whip and spur,
And minds its clamors less than soughing winds!
   BURBO. Now art thou Commodus again!
   COMMODUS.   No more—
But get thee to thy wine, and till to-night
Disport thyself, and find some seasoning
Against surprise and terror. Thou'rt a prince
Of mighty men, my Burbo, yet a man.
   BURBO. And thou art Hercules come back to us!
                         [*Exit* COMMODUS.
When in my closing palm I have his seal,
And asking's up—Oh, well!—'Tis very bad
When out of folly good cannot be had. [*Exit* BURBO.

COMMODUS

Enter CLEANDER.

CLEANDER. The Senate's mine [*laughing*]. Where Tully sat and piped
A butcher yawns and wipes his greasy brows.
The chair in which great Caius thrust aside
The crown thrice offered him, a hostler holds,
And with his boisterous *By the gods* decides
Debate, and settles policies to put
The world in harness. Goodly samples they
Of all the rest! Now will my Commodus
But make me Chief of his Pretorians,
The legions mine, and mine his guards at gate
And door, and mine to make him proof 'gainst points
And poisons, I will cast the riot loose—
But who is this comes tripping after me?

Enter a CHILD *as Cupid.*

CHILD. A letter, good my lord.
                     [CLEANDER *takes the letter.*
CLEANDER.   A woman's hand—
Chick, chick, a kiss!
  CHILD.   Thou good, thou best of men!
                         [CHILD *kisses him.*
CLEANDER. Whom serve you?
CHILD. The mistress Marcia.
CLEANDER.   Oh, when Marcia speaks,
The talking gods must bite their tongues and hear!—

Now what?   [*He reads the letter.*
    The Fates are good—another kiss!
Now back to her who sent you. Tell her come
To-day—to-morrow—when it pleases her.
No matter of the state, nor anything
Of gods or men, but it shall be postponed,
To her a secondary.   [*Exit* CHILD.
            Marcia sends
To ask if she may come and see me soon.
Perhaps—perhaps she's tired of Commodus—
Perhaps her sharper eyes have seen a sign
Portending change—perhaps Crispina hunts
Her to a last resort—perhaps—perhaps—
Enough! Let change what will, but this is true—
There ne'er was throne that had not room for two.
                                [*Exit.*

SCENE 2.—*A village street. Porch of an inn projecting into street.*

Enter MATERNUS. *He stops at a door under the porch.*

MATERNUS. 'Lo, here!

Enter LANDLORD.

LANDLORD. Your servant, please.

MATERNUS. I am tired, hungry, thirsty — what have you?

LANDLORD. Only the poorest, your goodness. I had

plenty—to-day three weeks ago—I think it was three weeks—my poor head, I lost it then, and it has hardly come back yet—a band of robbers—they said they belonged to the great Maternus, your graciousness—

MATERNUS. I'm a plain mechanic, friend, bound to Rome in hopes of finding work.

LANDLORD. No harm meant—Oh no! As I was saying—my poor head, it goes and comes so—to-day three weeks ago—I think it was three weeks—a band of robbers cleaned our village. They carried the inside of every house into the street. You should have seen what all they did!

MATERNUS. But I am hungry.

LANDLORD. Gracious excellency, I was about to say the thieves left me nothing but oatmeal and milk.

MATERNUS. Bring them—and haste.

LANDLORD. Yes, yes— [*Exit* LANDLORD.

Enter BACCHANTES. *They stop before the porch and sing. Villagers pour in from all sides.* MATERNUS *seats himself upon a bench, and the food is brought him. At close of the song,* QUEEN OF BACCHANTES *comes to the porch.*

QUEEN (*to* LANDLORD). O sleek and fat! Of your plenty, help us on our way.

LANDLORD. Your fairness, I have nothing. To-day three weeks ago—I think it was three weeks—

QUEEN. Nothing? You lie as only a landlord can.

THE SINGING BACCHANTES

UNIV. OF
CALIFORNIA

[*To* MATERNUS.] Your fare is humble. Are you of the road, like us?
MATERNUS. Yes.
QUEEN. Then of you, nothing.
[*She turns away, but comes back.*
Mercy! I forgot.
A mother, poor but good, and weary worn
With travel all afoot, is coming on,
With two fair children, bound to Rome to find
Her husband, there a soldier. If of store
You have to spare, a little give for her
And them; or if, like us, you have but small,
A very, very little then will do—
Oh, bare enough to buy a crust to feed
Three sparrows.—No? Ah, friend, had you a wife
To follow all your marching round the world—
A babe to toss its tiny arms about,
And cry your name—sweet, blue-eyed, cheek in blush
Of roses dipped—a boy to lift your spear,
And swear there ne'er was soldier like to you,
Nor any man so brave!—For such I beg.
MATERNUS (*affected*). Wilt thou indeed remember them?
QUEEN. I swear it by the holy gods.
MATERNUS. The Northman's hand is hard; not so his heart.
Take this to them. [*He gives her silver.*
QUEEN. A man to make a hero, although there was a tear upon his cheek. [*To* BACCHANTES.] And now,

my children, to the tambourines, for the honor of Cyprus. Care, begone!

[*Each unslings her tambourine, and they dance. At the conclusion* QUEEN *solicits gifts, in the midst of which curtain falls.*

Fourth Day

ACT IV

SCENE I.—ROME. *A gallery in the Imperial Palace.*

Enter CLEANDER *and* MARCIA.

MARCIA. I pray you use me plainly.
CLEANDER. Then I say Crispina goes to Capri.¹ Cæsar gave The order.
MARCIA. Well?
CLEANDER. They say the utmost wish Of souls at Capri is—[*laughing*] an obolus.
MARCIA. My hate disarms itself. I cannot laugh. She was his lawful wife; and something says In ear to me, a wife, if only she Be good and loving, bides near heaven's gate To let her husband in.
CLEANDER. But say that he Be bad?

---

¹ CRISPINA—wife of Commodus. Being taken in adultery, she was transported to the island of Capri, and there put to death by order of Commodus.

MARCIA. Then she is worse of being good.
My lord, a better wife had made the world
A better Cæsar.—Good my lord—
                    [*She draws nearer him.*
CLEANDER.   I hear—
I hold my breath to hear.
MARCIA.   There is a tale
I long have wished to tell thee; but the days
Seemed envious, and often as I asked
Them if 'twere time to tell it, offered doubts
That chilled the anxious wish, and left me still
Afraid, and to the morrow coldly bound.
        [*She rests her hand upon his shoulder.*
'Tis of a Phrygian boy. Wilt hear me now?
        [*He smiles, and bends his face nearer hers.*
In kindly humor once the Fates did chance
To see him where he followed after flocks
Of browsing sheep across a plain so wide
It filled its own horizon; then they had
Him brought to Rome, and in the palace yoked,
The Prince Imperial's mate; and thence the two,
In brotherhood, did grow so like and like
The shrew'est might not tell the first in wit,
Or any of the properties of men
In beardless youth. At last the lad a need
Of life became; so much that, wanting him,
Young Cæsar wanted eyes and ears and hands,
Nor was his perfect self. A teacher thus,

He too was equal taught; acquiring how
To govern men, which once attained does stir
The gods to jealousy, such knowledge 'tis.
  CLEANDER. Hush, hush!
[*He puts his arm about her.*
Go to, go to, I say! The plea
Of pretty maudler might not win you free
Of treason. Hush!
  MARCIA. Thou seest of whom I speak!
It is enough! O good my lord—my prince—
My Cæsar! Look you how the Roman world
Comes trundling to your hand. Reach and take it.
And then—
  CLEANDER. And then—what?
  MARCIA. Oh, then thou shalt be
The flower of men, and I a butterfly
To live upon thy sweets! I'll watch thy face
For signs of thought astir, and be its slave
Before the word receives it. To thy hand
I'll be as facile fingers ready taught
To answer every pulse of heart thou hast.
And thou shalt say when I can help thee best,
And prompt the mode, by labor, life or death
Indifferent.
  CLEANDER. The doors of sense all seem
To close upon me!—Oh, thou wert a star
With five clear rays; but now a sixth begins
To shine; and grow thou thus, the sky must be

Enlarged anew to hold thy flood of light.
        [*He kisses her passionately.*
Tell me but this—Is't perfect treaty now,
That we to end move on, the two as one?
    MARCIA. As ship and shadow go, and thou the ship.
        [*He takes her hand.*
    CLEANDER. A dainty hand, and small, to have such power
Of help to dizzy height; and qualitied
Divinely, that, by speechless tenderness,
And signs not more than writing on the air,
The ruffled feathers of suspicion it
Can instant lay, and even cast a man
In sleep of health profound to deeper sleep,
Which needs not health or any vanity,
Not even empire. Wouldst thou kill for me?
    MARCIA. Dost ask an oath?
    CLEANDER.   No, no—the love that needs
An oath to keep it true but taints the oath
In taking.—Look!   [*He shows her a tablet.*
        Whose name is this here writ?
    MARCIA. Commodus!
    CLEANDER.   Ay—at last—this warrant makes
Me his Pretorian Prefect. He is mine—
And Rome is mine! Dost hear? The mob let loose
On him to-day will make me first of kings,
And thou of women first. 'Tis said and sealed.
And now, my fair, a kiss—and then a kiss—

Then off to think what we must do to bring
Our wedded hopes to harbor.
    MARCIA.   Good, good-bye!
    CLEANDER. My queen!
    MARCIA.   Cæsar!—My gracious lord of lords!
                [*They embrace. Exit* CLEANDER.
An hour ago, with dread intent, and means
To put it into everlasting deed,
And he was terrible; but now is he
Self-given mine. The meed of a fool's tongue
Is a fool's death.—Away—to Cæsar next!   [*Exit.*

    SCENE 2.—*Road through a rocky pass.*

Enter BACCHANTES. *They cross from right to left. After them* MATERNUS, *his* WIFE *and* CHILDREN, *who stop.* MATERNUS *comes forward.*

    MATERNUS. No more of bleak inhospitable winds;
No more of dizzy passes under cliffs
Of threatening snow; for this is where the gods
Still keep their gardens fresh as in the hour
The sun first looked upon them—Italy,
The end of wandering! And hither speed
My comrades. In the valleys, by the shores
Of southward running streams, I hear them come,
Not needing beat of drum or bugle's blast
To tell me where they are. O Cybele!

As thou art mother of the poor and wronged,
Stay with us now!
  [*His wife comes to him, and lays her hand upon his arm.*
                    Ah, love, had you your will,
What would you?
  WIFE.   I would have you home again,
My arms around you thus.   [*She clasps his neck.*
  MATERNUS.   Not if you knew
We went to better fortune?
  WIFE.   So it is
With men. They will not learn that love is most
A woman wants, and give her that, and change
Is what she prays against.
  MATERNUS.   But you forget—
The cave was cold, and colder still the clime,
And to a land of roses now we come,
Where Summer year-long bides in purple tents,
Or on the vine-clad slopes keeps watch the while
The berries blushing turn to amber wine.
Give me your eyes—this way—there—call you that
A changeling's kiss? Oh, in the city's heart,
Fixed centre of the world, there is a house
Of marble out and marble in, where none
But master kings have dwelt and merry made;
And all its pillared gates and sculptured doors
Ajar do waiting stand for you and me,
And these our weary, weary little ones;

And we will enter in, and be at rest,
And call it ours, and with the great be great,
Yet happy each in other. Let us on.—
Hear you there?—Forward, boy, and sing for cheer.
[Exeunt, boy singing On to Rome.

Scene 3.—*Street in Rome. Noise of a riot in the distance.*

Enter Citizen in haste.

1 Citizen. Somebody's going to the mills for grinding. Should it be Cleander, good—for then the devil will have a chance to look at his other self. If Commodus—I'm not so certain as to him—a worse might come, and it asks not a doctor to say a simple fever's better than a compound one. [*Noise approaching.*] Ha, ha, ha! Let it be grinding for a mill or boiling for a pot, I'll not wait to see. [*Exit.*

Enter two other Citizens.

2 Citizen. They're on the other street.

3 Citizen. From the noise, I should say so. What's it all about?

2 Citizen. Oh, it's the worst yet!

3 Citizen. It must be very bad.

2 Citizen. I'll tell you. Burbo and our Cæsar had a quarrel. This one bragged how he had killed a thousand men in combat; that one, he said yes—

3 Citizen. How? Was it Cæsar said yes?

COMMODUS

2 CITIZEN. No, Burbo—Burbo said Cæsar had killed a thousand men; he knew, for he had kept the score; but, he said, when it came to dying, the Romans who were of the lot had always been the most cowardly. Then Cæsar he laid him a wager, half his empire 'gainst the bully's sword, that he'd prove him false. [*Outbreak of noise.*]—Just hear that!

3 CITIZEN. Well, how did Cæsar set about it?

2 CITIZEN. Oh, that was easy enough for Cæsar! He gave a feast—with all the empty bellies on the street, there's been a plenty in the palace—he gave a feast, I say, and had the hostages and ambassadors from all the nations to Rome go eat and drink with him; and then—

3 CITIZEN. And then?

2 CITIZEN. Well, he poisoned them—

3 CITIZEN. Oh, holy gods!

2 CITIZEN. And told them of it—and while they were dying, he and Burbo looked on to see how they behaved.

3 CITIZEN. Was there a Roman amongst them?

2 CITIZEN. The Master of the Feast served comparison for us.

3 CITIZEN. And he died?

2 CITIZEN. He too died.

3 CITIZEN. Which won?

2 CITIZEN. Neither. Burbo he swore by his Gauls—

3 CITIZEN. Yes, he's a Gaul himself.

2 CITIZEN. Commodus he swore by his Roman; and between them they've tickled the common throat with

a feather, and now these go making tubs of themselves
to carry the gorge to Jove.
3 CITIZEN. Let's join them.
2 CITIZEN. And share the plunder.
3 CITIZEN. Here—this way, this way! [*Exeunt.*

Enter MARCIA *hurriedly.*

MARCIA (*pausing to listen*). Oh, a most hideous, loud-
  mouthed, roaring beast
They make of it! I did not think to be
So much afraid of them. Were it but bread
They want—
  [*She unclasps her bracelets and throws them away.*
          I here give ovensful to such
As find the trinketry, which, sooth to say,
Endangers me.   [*She moves on, but stops again.*
          I heard my Cæsar's name—
And there, Cleander's! Oh, a blasphemous
Conjunction, yet of excellent effect,
Reminding me the monsters are abroad
For blood as well as bread, and I must haste—
But footsteps! Holy gods defend me now!—
My friends the Senators—I breathe again!
               [*She covers her head.*

Enter POMPEIANUS, BURRHUS, *and* ANTONINUS.

BURRHUS. What woman's this?
POMPEIANUS. Her air ill suits the hour.

ANTONINUS. Hast thou a husband in yon discontent?
MARCIA. I have no husband.
ANTONINUS. Well, thou hast a home?
MARCIA. And if I have?
ANTONINUS. Then haste, and get thee there.
Or if thou think'st to test the pack we hear
For favors, hie thee to a tannery,
And in its foulness curry till thou'rt green.
Thy gown is all too fresh.
MARCIA. Most excellent,
Good gentlemen, am I not known to you?
[*She uncovers her face.*
BURRHUS. Aha! The mistress Marcia!
POMPEIANUS. So it is!
ANTONINUS. A day to daunt whoever walks in it.
What dost thou here?
MARCIA. I go to serve the cause
You most affect.
ANTONINUS. Too late! The cause is dead—
Stamped out by Cæsar. Think of that he did
Last night! The hostages whom we have kept
In pledge for treaties, eldest sons of kings
And friendly princes—poor, homesick, forlorn,
And helpless, therefore sacred public guests—
He slew them! And the heads of embassies—
Where are they? Vile enough had they been claimed
By cold inexorable policy,
And shuffled off in fact for country's sake;

To kill them drinking to our Roman gods,
And of their dying make a butcher's jest,
Must leave us damned and godless!
    MARCIA.   Good my lords,
I see there is a difference between
The loves of men and women. Comes a cloud,
A little cloud, to drop a passing shade
Upon it, yours turns sick and given up;
But ours would live although the sun at noon
Were stricken out—would live, and in the night,
The unrelieved darkness worse than night,
Pilot its object home.   [*Shouting again, but fainter.*
                          Does not the noise
Recede from us?
    POMPEIANUS.   I think so.
    BURRHUS.   They have turned
Towards the palace.
    MARCIA.   Haste—run after them—
    ANTONINUS. Nay, even youth is laggard till it knows
What waits it at the goal.
    MARCIA.   You are most kind
To deal so gently with my hasty speech
And manner. I will mend them, so you bear
With me, and render you a simple tale
Of that now going to such dismal end.
My lords did one day stop to speak with me
Of Roman griefs—
    POMPEIANUS.   We well remember it.

MARCIA. The charges which my lords then left in trust
With me to Cæsar's self I truly gave;
But he did laugh, and put them lightly off,
And shower Cleander all the more with gifts
And honors rich with power; until at last
He made him general of all his guards,
Both those in camp, and those who keep his gates
And inner doors—and now conclusions come.
Within the hour I heard the traitor swear
The risen sun should see him first of kings;
And sending out, he straightway set the mob
To trumpeting. And then were Cæsar lost,
But that I ran and warned him, and with tears
And prayers to reinforce my argument,
Had Burbo and his swordsmen man the gates
In place of doubtful guards; and doing so,
By happy chance, they shut the traitor in,
And there he is.
BURRHUS. Oh, excellent, and most
Duteous!
MARCIA. Yes, my lords, 'twas Cæsar saved!—
And now, will you but help me, I will do
The other half of duty—that to Rome.
POMPEIANUS. There is contagion in her confidence!
MARCIA. You know Fadilla?
BURRHUS. Ay, we know her well.
MARCIA. See how the bad does often mix itself

In our affairs to give them happy turn.
Commodus did but now refuse the prayer
I made him on my knees, that Burbo take
Cleander's head, and serve it to the mob;
So should the mutiny be quickest closed.
One hope remains—Fadilla's voice with mine
May win what mine alone could not.

    ANTONINUS.   She must
Forgive him first.

    MARCIA.   Ah, good my lords, she is
A Christian now, and dying.

    ANTONINUS.   How then canst
Thou have a hope? Her beauty gone, she may
Not move him more.

    MARCIA.   My lord, I know him best.
The other self, in him not less than us,
Sets racking devils on him in his sleep.
And not infrequent I have seen him from
His dreams come rushing back to wakeful life,
And cower behind his outstretched quivering hands,
The while he cried to her by proper name,
As children cry release from punishment—
Is't not enough, my lords? Or shall I say
I too have known the sickness called remorse,
Which by its stings and stabs in oddest times,
And modes immedicable, does but prove
The conscience in us yet. I know its signs
And gestures, look and voice, its turns and tricks,

COMMODUS

And when its spasms strike, like arrows sped,
The sore and tender places of the soul;
And more, my lords, to make confession dumb,
I know that pardon is its only cure.
    ANTONINUS (*aside*). She may be right. [*Aloud.*] Fair
      mistress, count us friends
To your intent; and what we can we will
To help you.
    MARCIA.   Oh! it is a simple part,
But honorable. Only gain me time
To see Fadilla, and with her repass
The palace gate before the war arrives
And shuts us out.
    BURRHUS.   That has an easy look.
I know a lane to take us to the front,
And there we'll speak until the mob refuse
To hear us.
    POMPEIANUS. Let us go—I never thought
To run again.
    BURRHUS.   Nor I.
    POMPEIANUS.   Is that the way?
    BURRHUS. Follow me—here!
      [*Exeunt* BURRHUS *and* POMPEIANUS. ANTONINUS
      takes MARCIA's *hand.*
    ANTONINUS. Have I been rude, then much I crave
      your grace.
Rome by a woman saved would still be Rome.
                      [*Exeunt.*

SCENE 4.—*Chamber in the Palace.* COMMODUS *upon a couch playing with a lute.* COURTIERS *in attendance. Noise of a battle heard at intervals outside.*

1 COURTIER. Hark, how the tumult deepens at the gate!
2 COURTIER. 'Tis bloody war.'
3 COURTIER.   But see! There lies he calm As in the universe such dreadful thing As danger were not.   [*Uproar without.*
   O great Jupiter!
COMMODUS. Here, one of you.
1 COURTIER.   He calls—stay, I'll attend.
   [*He goes to* COMMODUS.

---

[1] A famine was the cause of the riot which resulted in Cleander's fall.
—CREVIER. *History of the Roman Emperors.*
   To the same effect GIBBON says:
   "Pestilence and famine contributed to fill up the measure of the calamities of Rome. The first could only be imputed to the just indignation of the gods; but a monopoly of corn, supported by the riches and power of the minister (*Cleander*), was considered as the immediate cause of the second. The popular discontent, after it had long circulated in whispers, broke out in the assembled circus. The people quitted their favorite amusements for the more delicious pleasure of revenge, rushed in crowds towards a palace in the suburbs — one of the imperial retirements — and demanded with clamors the head of the public enemy.... The tumult became a regular engagement, and threatened a general massacre. The pretorians at length gave way, oppressed with numbers, and the tide of popular fury returned with redoubled violence against the gates of the palace where Commodus lay, dissolved in luxury, and alone unconscious of the civil war."—GIBBON. Chapter IV.

COMMODUS. You spoke of some Bacchantes come to
  Rome.   [*Quick swell of the fight.*
2 COURTIER. Hear him! Ye gods!
3 COURTIER.   The battle holds my ear.
2 COURTIER. Is't courage?
3 COURTIER.   No; 'tis madness.
COMMODUS.   You did speak,
I say, of dancing girls from Cyprus come,
And noising all the town.
  1 COURTIER.   Yes, good my lord.
COMMODUS. Have them engaged for me.
  1 COURTIER.   It shall be done.
                       [*Exit* COURTIER.
2 COURTIER. Oh, if 'tis madness, he will die in it!
3 COURTIER. He has us all to keep him company.
                       [*Uproar continues.*

      Enter MARCIA *and* FADILLA.

MARCIA. O Cæsar—dear my Cæsar!
                       [*She kneels by him.*
COMMODUS.   Why so pale?

      Enter 1 COURTIER *in alarm.*

2 COURTIER. How goes the fight?
  1 COURTIER.   The guards retreat within
The gates, which hardly to their hinges cling.
  MARCIA. Dear, dear my lord, he says the gates give
  way.

COMMODUS. Thou foolish! [*To* COURTIER.] Hence,
and bid Cleander come.

MARCIA.[1] O Cæsar, 'tis of him I wish to speak;
Nor I alone.   [*She takes* FADILLA *to him.*
             This other has a word
I pray you, Cæsar, hear.

COMMODUS (*sitting up.*) Death ne'er himself
So perfect looked!—And with my father's eyes,
So crying piteous I would turn from them,
But cannot.—Ah! to upbraid me, com'st thou?

FADILLA. O Cæsar—brother! I have come from calm
Of cloister life, a Christian, prayerful
For all the sinful world. To serve and save
You I am here.

COMMODUS.   Thou!

FADILLA.   Well indeed the last
Of life were this wise spent!
             [*She staggers. He rises and catches her.*

COMMODUS.   Nay, lean on me.

FADILLA. My brother, all Rome armed is at thy gates,

---

[1] "He (*Commodus*) would have perished in this supine security had not two women, his eldest sister (*Fadilla*) and Marcia, the most favored of his concubines, ventured to break into his presence. Bathed in tears, and with dishevelled hair, they threw themselves at his feet, and with all the passing eloquence of fear, discovered to the affrighted Emperor the crimes of the minister, the rage of the people, and the impending ruin, which in a few minutes would have burst over his palace and person. Commodus started from his dream of pleasure, and commanded that the head of Cleander should be thrown out to the people. The desired spectacle instantly appeased the tumult."—GIBBON. Chapter IV.

And thou art lost unless Cleander die.
Hear what he has done. [*Increase of noise without.*
Hear the people cry
For justice on the traitor.
COMMODUS.   Jupiter!
And this from her?—And with her dying breath?
   FADILLA. I charge him so, and bid the battle bear
Me witness. Know thou now—God grant it soon
Enough!—this madness of revolt hath come
Of wrongs by him devised to break the heart
Of Roman patience.

   Enter BURBO *in full armor.*
BURBO.   Hail, Cæsar! I bring
A call for you.
         [COMMODUS *gives* FADILLA *to* MARCIA.
   COMMODUS. What, beaten? Thou and they
Whom yesterday I would have put afield
Against the Julian larks? But now in flight
Before a mob?
   BURBO. The mob? [*Laughing.*] Tush! Bare of face
And throat and body they, and fighting them
Is merely taking step, with shield advanced,
And thrusting thus—and thus—an ancient trick!
To us the mob! But, Cæsar, I do bid
You wake to treachery.
   COMMODUS.   To treachery?

BURBO. The Prefect of thy guard' against the need
Withholds his legions.
COMMODUS.   Ye immortal gods,
Let loose and blast the ingrate with thy quick
Consuming fires! Oh, I remember now
With what ado of love, and plausible
Fair-seeming show of duty, he did win
The Prefecture! Of mobs he'd make an end—
This one outside my gates he'd tread in mire
Of blood so deep 'twould ne'er take root again—
And I did sign!—Fadilla, have thy will—
His fate is overdue. [*To* BURBO.] Where keeps he now?
BURBO. Upon the roof, my Cæsar, triply fenced
With guards which should be thine.
COMMODUS.   A thing for swift
And certain deed!—Go bring his head to me!
Hearest thou? Speed!—Ay—but—would I were by
To see his dying!—Burbo, do thou watch,
And note his changes—hear what last he says—
Observe if light or hard his parting be,
Or brave or fearful. Get thee wings. Away!
MARCIA. With all its dripping, I do kiss thy hand.
[*She kisses* BURBO's *hand.*

---

[1] *Prefect of the Guard*—literally, General of the Pretorian Legions.
Cleander degraded the office to pave the way to it himself. He made and unmade such Prefects at his pleasure; he had one for five days, and another for six hours. At last he obtained the place himself.—CREVIER. *History of the Roman Emperors.*

COMMODUS. Not cowering quails, but royal game,
  Death hunts
With baying hounds to-day. [*To* COURTIERS.] Bring
  sword and shield!
I'll meet him armed, and die, if die I must,
In sort to live a braggart's boast upon
His grinning lips.—Be off—nor loiter so!
  [*A* COURTIER *runs out.* COMMODUS *turns to* FADILLA.
Her gaze does turn my mood to tearful grief,
And teach a love which I have lived to this
Unknowing.—Good friends, bear her to yon couch.
  [ATTENDANTS *obey him. He follows them, and stands
    by her.*
This is not dying—or was never death
So gentle—or 'tis meant to show me what
It should be. Stay—a moment ere thou go—
And tell me I am pardoned.
  FADILLA.   As would Christ—
Forgiven!   [FADILLA *dies.*

Enter BURBO *with* CLEANDER's *head.*

BURBO.   Lo, Cæsar! I bring you peace!
  [COMMODUS *takes the head and holds it up before him.*
MARCIA. My lord, a wondrous specious tongue it had.
Thy workmen coin not silver pieces half
So artfully as it when pleased did coin
The basest lies.

COMMODUS

[*Tumult without.* COMMODUS *takes the head to a table, and, setting it on the neck, draws a chair before it.*

COMMODUS.   For this together grew
We statured men.   Open, eyes!   Answer, tongue!
Tell me of that which was so lately life.
Where is it now? and what, if 'tis at all?
Can it be down, some serving quality,
In lawless current blowing with the air,
A breath's sweet virtue here, or there a blight
Of poison?   Dost thou hear me?   Or did Death,
With grim compassion touched, open a gate
On noiseless hinges swung, and let it hence
To live a better being or a worse?
I do bid thee—I, Cæsar—break the law
Which 'gainst me speechless locks thy purple lips—
Yes or no—speak!—Is there another life?
                                    [*Tumult without.*
MARCIA.   O dear my lord! [*clasping his knees*]—my
   Cæsar—save thyself
This favoring time.
   COMMODUS (*to the head*).   I lifted thee above
Thy station.   Nay, I bent the stubborn world,
And set thy foot upon it.   At thy word,
In whisper said, the millions crouching quaked.
Now not a sign?—Go to, thou thrice damned clod!
Enrich some lentil patch of teeming earth,
Or feed a weed, or paint a lily's cup,

Of uses last.—My Burbo, thine it is—
Take now, and throw it to the swine without.
'Twill stay their grunting for the time at least.—
[*To* COURTIER.] My sword.—Stay, Burbo! Died he like a man?
BURBO. Ay, like a man, my Cæsar.
COMMODUS.   This one died
Forgiving me. What man would do as much?
[*Exit* BURBO *with the head.* COMMODUS *remains by the couch, playing with the point of his sword and looking at* FADILLA.

Enter COURTIER.

COURTIER. The mob is gone.
COMMODUS.   I thought so. — This poor dead
One shall to lovers of her sect, that they
May bury her. Thou, Marcia, shalt attend
The rites.
MARCIA. I will, my lord.[1]
COMMODUS.   Put up, good sword;
For yet I have a time to ripen in.
[*To* COURTIER.] The Fates relent. Return it whence it came.   [*Curtain falls.*

---

[1] The Christians are said to have enjoyed great peace under Commodus, credit for which is given to Marcia.—CREVIER. *History of the Roman Emperors.*

"YES OR NO—SPEAK!—IS THERE ANOTHER LIFE?"

Fifth Day

ACT V

SCENE I.—*Under the walls of Rome.* MARCUS *and other* CAPTAINS *seated.*

Enter MATERNUS.

MATERNUS. Hail, comrades! Hail, and hearty cheer to each
And all of you!
   [*They rise and press him with their greetings.*
               The morn before the *Nones*
Of April this; and there, the trysting gate
Of old Flaminius. Thanks, each to each,
And thanks to Cybele, and solemn vows.—
And now, my brothers—such you are in faith
As well as fortune—unto other time,
The day of golden leisure, let us pass
All mention of the road, nor think of else
Than that which waits us urgent to be done—
And of our soldiers first.
   MARCUS.   They swarm the streets.
   MATERNUS. Have they the meeting-place?

MARCUS. They have.
MATERNUS. And arms and uniforms?
MARCUS. They'll come for them to-night.
MATERNUS. Have they the word?
MARCUS. Ay, captain.
MATERNUS. You know, my Marcus, I do rest on you
As on myself.—They smiled, I think you said?
Was that their spirit? Did their faces flush?
Spake they quick, sharp? And when they took your hand,
Thought you if closed their fingers thus—and thus—
As itching for the sword? You know there are
Who dash you with their doubts, and crawling go
To tasks heroic. Them I stamp as vile.
For look you all, my brethren, they have want
Of minds resolved; and in the heated seethe
Of action, when the winging chances all
The fiercer fan their pinched and fear-washed cheeks,
And comes the crisis with its thunder-clap,
They stop to think, and with themselves debate;
And then the gods do hiss, and slip their dooms,
And shoot them swift into the weakling's hell.
MARCUS. I judged them good of spirit.
MATERNUS.   Stay they so,
My captains, then will we a deed to sound
All Wonder's brassy pipes.—But part we now.
1 CAPTAIN. Hold, comrades — a word. There must always be a Cæsar. Will not Maternus do for us?

2 CAPTAIN. Why not?

1 CAPTAIN. If that's your mind, let's say so, and give him hands on it.

CAPTAINS. Ay, every hand! Live Maternus!
 [*All give him their hands, and with such speeches as,* We are with you!—Count on us!

MATERNUS. Again, good rest, my brethren.
 [*Exeunt all but* MARCUS.

MARCUS. When with my hand he played, I thought
 I saw
Suspicion in his eyes. A little while,
And he and I were one; but now—to brush
Great Cæsar from his throne! I'll watch a time
To loose the feathers in his soaring wing.
Truly as men get up in dreams of state,
The loves they once did cherish turn to hate. [*Exit.*

SCENE 2.—*A royal chamber.* COMMODUS *seated upon a couch. Children upon the couch asleep.*

COMMODUS. How soft the air! A feather dropt would
 plunge
It like a stone; and all my senses swim
In it immerged, uncertain where to find
Their qualities, whether here on this shore
Of life awake, or there on that of life
Asleep. I'll call the truants back.—But soft!
 [*He looks at the children.*

They are so still! All sleep should be like theirs,
A going to some dusky land to have
Ourselves made o'er again.
[*He moves quietly to one side.*
Ho, there—without!

Enter COURTIER.

COURTIER. I thought my lord did call.
COMMODUS. What is the hour?
[*He resumes seat upon the couch.*
COURTIER. The sun is up, my lord.
COMMODUS. Have I so stretched
The night? A peaceful night it must have been.
I did not even dream. From such a sleep
To pleasure—then from pleasure back to sleep—
I want no more of being.—What is set
For me to-day?
COURTIER. The Masque of Cybele.
COMMODUS. 'Tis on ere this.
COURTIER. They say 'twas ne'er so fine.
The city joins the sport with loyal will.
COMMODUS. The wounds a public takes heal wondrous
    fast.
A holiday will cure them.—Pass we that.
COURTIER. The dancing girls from Cyprus wait your will.
COMMODUS. Have they been seen?
COURTIER. Ay.
COMMODUS. Tell me how they look.

COURTIER. My lord has seen young leopards at their play,
And in their grace of action quite forgot
Their fiercer moods of nature. So these girls.
At sight of them in frolic of the dance,
I only asked to see again and soon.
  COMMODUS. Well, have them ready.
  COURTIER.   When?
  COMMODUS.   By the third hour.
  COURTIER. Where, my lord?
  COMMODUS.   In our hall of state—and bring
Me word when time is up.
  COURTIER.   I will, my lord.
  COMMODUS. And hark! I want the lazy meanwhile filled.
  COURTIER. Music, my lord?
  COMMODUS.   Not music; for 'tis sleep's
Best minister, and I have come from sleep
But now.
  COURTIER. My lord must name what most he wants.
  COMMODUS. Then bring me wine, and in a crystal cup—
Red wine alive with Ætna's lava-glow.
                     [COURTIER *looks at the children.*
  COURTIER. Is it your pleasure that they be removed?
  COMMODUS. Come nearer, friend—I would not waken
    them.
In your ear. You may some day do a deed
To strike you from the list which Slumber keeps
Of those it loves. Go not to doctors then;
Nor send witch-women to the fields for herbs;

But find where children haunt, and there unman,
And with them laugh and play, and when at last
They lay them down to rest, do you the same.
Then Innocence, which keeps the golden key
Of sleep, and waits on them, will wait on you—
A happy, happy time it is for them,
And it were pitiful were we to rob
Them of it.   Come, then—gently—[*he turns to children at the moment of exit*]—so.—Adieu!   [*Exeunt.*

SCENE 3.—*Street.   People passing in holiday garb, and masked.*

Enter MATERNUS *and* MARCUS *in Pretorian uniforms, and armed, helms, swords, and shields.*

MATERNUS. My Marcus, where we sat awhile ago,
Our people, going by, saluted us,
Until it seemed to me the very air
Did pall and hang o'erweighted with the word—
Mors! Mors! I think we could have something had
Less loud with warning. Marked you e'er a bee
In humming flight but of its sting you thought?—
Howbeit, 'tis an error too far gone
For mending, if we would.—What is the hour?
  MARCUS. I think it is the third.
  MATERNUS.   Art thou not slow?
Or is it that my patience wears a spur?
            [*He shades his eyes and looks upward.*

COMMODUS

I saw the heralds of the sun at dawn,
When first they shook their lances in the sky;
Then came the sun himself; and as he rose,
A single cloud of more than fleecy white,
Asleep above me like a ship becalmed,
Gave sudden start, and, ship-like, softly sailed
A-down to him. Some god did then suggest
My fortune in the cloud. I stood to see
What came of it; and as they nearer drew,
The cloud did slowly change from white to pink,
And then to rosy red; a veil of flame,
At last it hid the glorious burning disk,
And in a vermeil shade I wondering stood.
An instant—and again the brightness broke,
And upward rose the sun, and onward sailed
The cloud—on—on—until, in perfect peace,
It vanished, purpling in the morning sky—
And I did cry for joy.
                    [*A* SOLDIER *in Pretorian garb goes by.*
   SOLDIER.   *Mors!*
   MATERNUS.   There—didst hear,
My Marcus?
   MARCUS.   He is for the rendezvous.
   MATERNUS. Doubtless—and so, by this, are all of ours.
I fancy them on every pave in Rome
Towards the palace faced. Let us the same.
                                    [*They face about.*
   MARCUS. Some masquers come!

MATERNUS. They make the street alive.
[*The two draw aside while a procession passes, shouting, singing, and with trumpets and banners, and in grotesque disguises.*
MARCUS. Say you we fall in as a part of them?
MATERNUS. Yes, I am ready.—Oh, ye holy gods,
Who truly love the brave, go with us now! [*Exeunt.*

SCENE 4.—*Hall of state in Imperial Palace. Throne in centre, curtained right and left.*

Enter OFFICERS, *with lion's skin and club of Hercules.*
OFFICERS. Make way for Cæsar! Cæsar comes—make way!

Enter other OFFICERS, *and after them* COURTIERS, GLADIATORS, *and* CHARIOTEERS. BURBO *conspicuous. After them,* COMMODUS *in Pretorian uniform,* MARCIA *on his arm. With her he ascends the throne.*
COMMODUS (*to* MARCIA). Shall they begin?
MARCIA. If 'tis your pleasure, good my lord.
COMMODUS (*to* OFFICERS). Bid them come.

Enter QUEEN OF BACCHANTES, *and kneels before* COMMODUS.
QUEEN. O mighty Cæsar! Cyprus sends her love
To you, and there was never love like hers.
[*She rises and claps her hands. Music. Enter* BACCHANTES, *as priestesses of Aphrodite, and dance.*

Enter MATERNUS *and* MARCUS.

MATERNUS (*aside*). Accursed tyrant! Art thou met at last?
And as I prayed? Upon thy curtained throne?—
Amidst thy guards?—In lap degenerate?—
Set round with trinketry forbidden kings
And common gods? O happy, happy chance!
My Marcus, calm thy joy, as I will mine,
And let us to the dais with air of ease
To vouch us of the guard, and here of right.—
Thy sword—be jealous of the scabbard's clasp.
   MARCUS (*aside*). 'Tis ready—free.
   MATERNUS (*aside*). Remember, mine the hand
To strike the blow; and then, the freeze of fear
Upon them—sovereign moment when the gods
Do give the many to the cherished few!—
Back to the gates run thou, and call on ours,
And show them where their oft-dreamt joyance lies.
Let's done with words—let's on!
   MARCUS (*aside*).   I do believe
Him fortune-favored! It is time for me
To make a choice. Yon fellow looks as he
Were Cæsar born. He has the throne and odds—
I'll take to him.
   [*As they advance*, MARCUS *speaks to a* COURTIER.
        My friend, love you your king?

COURTIER. Who questions?
MARCUS.   *Mors!*
COURTIER.   *Mors!* What!—A stranger thou!—
Ho, Burbo!—Cæsar!—Here is mystery—
Treachery.—Guard, guard!
   [*Confusion. Women scream—guards rush from behind
   the curtains, and post themselves around the throne.*
   COMMODUS *rises.* MATERNUS *draws his sword.*
MATERNUS.   Oh! thou traitor, less
To me than universal humankind,
As thou didst call on death, death shalt thou have—
Ay, with godsend quick to hell!   [*He stabs* MARCUS.
MARCUS.   Cæsar saved—
Maternus lost!   [*Dies.*
MATERNUS.   Lost! Oh! the world is lost!
And hope's sweet promises! and martial dreams
Of helmèd war, and conquests empire-crowned!—
And Oh, poor, poor wife! This the meed òf all
Thy toil and faithfulness?—But boots it naught
So Cæsar keeps me instant company.
                         [*He clears a space.*
Gladiators—guards—Cæsar! Look—behold
Maternus!
   BURBO.   Thou Maternus?—'Tis—'tis so!
My Cæsar—Cæsar, 'ware, and out with sword,
Or take you hence on wings. I know the man—
One mother bore us both.
   COMMODUS.   The insolent!

DEATH OF MATERNUS

Set on him all   Dost hear?   His life or yours!
    [GUARDS *hang back.* BURBO *snatches a sword, advances towards* MATERNUS, *but falters.*
BURBO. His eyes are gleaming godlike—terrible!
MATERNUS. I know you, Burbo — mother's youngest born—
And by her blood in us the very same,
And by my senior's right, I bid you turn,
As she would have you—turn, and that way strike
With me!   [*He advances.* BURBO *retreats.*
    A cruel Roman hand did tear
Us from her arms, in dying vainly stretched
To hold us fast; and 'neath a Roman foot
Our free-born fighting father death-struck died.
There she is—Rome the Vast—the Each and All—
Imbruted into one; and here are we,
With ready swords, and oft-tried, practised hands,
And fire-eyed, frenzied Hate to trumpet us.—
End of him is end of her.—Forward both!
                              [BURBO *gives back.*
BURBO. Back, back, I say, and I will be your fence
Against the world—or Rome—or Cæsar's self.
    MATERNUS. A base-grown, sodden tongue to speak me so!
That way a barren death; and this way death,
But death with glory as a stop to pain.
Choose, I say, and quick—Commodus or me!
    [*He kills* BURBO, *and throws himself upon the* GUARD.

MARCIA. The guards give way! O Cæsar, let us fly!
For see, his look is deadly as his sword.
     [*She throws her arms about him.*
 COMMODUS. Never! A Cæsar cannot fly from clash
Of reddening blades. Woman, loose thy arms!—
Bring sword for me! A thousand such I've slain;
Now this one comes at noon of fighting time
To swell the measure of my rugged boast.
Give me a sword!—Or strike—quick—well done there!
Habet—hoc habet! Up thumbs merciless!
 MATERNUS. Oh! Oh! I stop at heart! Night comes
  apace!
And life good fortune joins in farewell flight.
Done for am I! But he—O doomful gods!
Shall he escape?—of all this breathing world
The topmost curse!
    [*With last effort, he gains the throne.*
    Late—too late—at my feet—
     [*He falls blindly on the step.*
Darkness! O damned Cæsar! Take thou—this!
   [*He dashes the sword into the throne and dies.*

CURTAIN FALLS

www.ingramcontent.com/pod-product-compliance
Lightning Source LLC
Chambersburg PA
CBHW020847160426
43192CB00007B/821